CURTAINS?

THE FUTURE OF THE ARTS IN AMERICA

· ·

MICHAEL M. KAISER

BRANDEIS UNIVERSITY PRESS *Waltham, Massachusetts*

BRANDEIS UNIVERSITY PRESS

An imprint of University Press of New England

www.upne.com

Manufactured in the United States of America

Designed by Richard Hendel

Typeset in Utopia and Transat by Passumpsic Publishing

Library of Congress Cataloging-in-Publication Data

Kaiser, Michael M., 1953–

Curtains? : the future of the arts in America / Michael M. Kaiser.

   pages   cm

ISBN 978-1-61168-703-3 (cloth : alk. paper)—

ISBN 978-1-61168-704-0 (ebook)

1. Performing arts—United States. I. Title.

PN1582.U6K35   2015

790.2—dc23   2014023652

5 4 3 2

For my parents,

HAROLD *and* MARION KAISER,

who taught me to think ahead

CONTENTS

PREFACE

I am an arts manager because when I was four years old my parents took my siblings and me to see *The Music Man,* starring Barbara Cook as Marian the librarian. When she sang "Goodnight, My Someone," standing on the porch of her house, one could suddenly see through the wall of the house and watch Amaryllis play the piano. What magic made the house become transparent? I was hooked.

Since that moment, I have believed in the power of the arts to inspire, educate, and entertain. People in every culture draw and sing and dance. The need to express oneself is innate to human beings. It cannot be ignored, submerged or repressed for very long. Artists need to create beautiful and meaningful works. It is not a choice, it is a requirement.

The arts are necessary for every community's health and well-being. No great civilization can be sustained without the joy and the release provided by the arts. Only totalitarian societies limit art-making and such societies fail to endure, in part, because their people are denied an open, honest, creative outlet.

I remain convinced that any arts organization that does good work can be vibrant and healthy and sustainable. There is demand for great art and there is support available for the work of great artists and there always will be.

While I am confident there will always be art and artists in our world, however, I am less optimistic about the future of organized arts institutions: the opera, theater, ballet, and modern dance companies, the symphony orchestras and museums that currently present the vast majority of work created by professional artists. While there will always be art, I fear there will not always be the wide range of organized and professional arts venues, producers, and presenters that we currently enjoy.

My concern does not result simply from the difficult and extended period of economic instability we have recently endured. I am not a Depression-era child and I maintain a remarkably positive outlook on the potential for healthy arts organizations in any environment. (That's why I was willing to lead four virtually bankrupt arts organizations over the past thirty years.) Nor am I one in the chorus of voices intoning, "The arts model is broken." Many arts organizations that were managed and governed well during the recent recession remain healthy and should continue to be vibrant in the future if they enjoy strong leadership from board and staff.

The arts model is not broken. But the poor implementation of this model in an increasingly difficult environment causes me concern. Only a very few arts organizations are managed well, with consistent vigor and focus. Too many of them do little or no real planning. These institutions fail to produce interesting art, do not know how to market or raise funds, are governed by weak or ineffective boards, have failed to exploit new technologies wisely, and are clumsy about embracing supporters, both old and new. And while many of these organizations got by in the past, surviving the bumps and bruises, I fear their path will become ever more perilous. I am not optimistic that such institutions will exist two decades from now.

This pessimism arises from my experience with evaluating industries and the ways in which they mature. Before I became an arts manager, I was a business consultant who specialized in industry evolution. I studied dozens of industries—from jet engines to computers to automobiles—and learned how they changed and developed over time. I evaluated the impact of new technologies and studied how new modes of distribution changed industry dynamics. I analyzed how competitive pressures evolved as product lines changed, and how buyers became more powerful as specialty products turned into commodities. I even wrote two books on these topics.

My experiences consulting to a range of corporations in a myriad of industries, coupled with my observations over thirty years in arts management, have created a deep-seated discomfort with the current state of the art world. The many trends at work now are going to change our arts ecology forever. We have been fortunate to live in a remarkable era of arts accessibility, a true golden age. But it is coming to an end.

As I look twenty years into the future, I remain optimistic that those arts organizations that do things consistently well — the ones that create great and exciting art, that market effectively, that gather strong families of donors, audience members, and board members — will thrive.

But trends in technology, demographics, government support, and arts education are working against us. It is going to be increasingly difficult to thrive, or even survive, as an arts organization in the coming decades. There will be winners, for sure, but I am equally certain there will be a larger group of losers.

I know that many of my peers will disagree vehemently with my projections, and I fervently hope I am wrong. But I received similar reactions from executives at IBM and General Motors in the 1980s, when I suggested that their industries were changing in ways that would cause them major challenges. I had hoped to motivate change rather than scorn, but I failed.

I pray I am more successful this time around.

CURTAINS?

AMERICA THE BEAUTIFUL

. . . .

THE ARTS EXPLOSION,

. . . .

1950-2000

Those of us who were born in the United States of America in the decade following World War II have lived charmed lives. Our world has continuously changed and expanded in remarkable and magical ways. Most of us are more educated, wealthier, and better traveled than our parents. We were born in the age of television and have lived into the age of Netflix and Hulu. We witnessed the development of computers and lived into the age of iPads. Wary of long-distance telephone charges as children, we now speak at will, and at very low cost, on our smart phones. That is, when we speak at all, because we can e-mail and text to anyone at any time at almost no cost. Along the way we adopted, then discarded, fax machines, vcrs, cordless telephones, and numerous other gadgets that seemed like revelations when they were introduced and now seem merely quaint.

Our lives have expanded in other ways. We now travel everywhere, at relatively low cost. Airline ticket prices have fallen 40 percent since the 1950s. In 1958, 38 million people flew; fifty years later, that number was 809 million! We eat foods from every corner of the earth. I didn't taste pizza until I was ten years old; our children know the difference between sushi and sashimi. Where we once read a daily newspaper, we now access our information in real time: even twenty-four-hour news stations struggle to keep market share when so many of us get our news online, faster than it can be produced for television. We used to buy expensive encyclopedias; now we use Wikipedia for free. Instead of visiting a library to research a school paper, students now log on and search, then cut and paste.

These technological changes have been accompanied by earth-shaking social changes. We have lived through efforts to secure civil rights, women's rights, reproductive rights, and gay rights. (Hard as it might be for many younger people to imagine, there was even a battle to secure the right to divorce.) And while we still have much to accomplish, we now live in a more equitable society than we were born into.

Much else has changed over the past seventy years. For those of us who care about the arts — and a remarkable number do — there has been an explosion in the accessibility and diversity of live performances and visual arts exhibitions. Except for a few of our venerable museums, orchestras, and opera companies, most of the arts organizations in today's United States were formed after World War II. With some notable exceptions, many of our most famous modern dance companies, theater organizations, ballet companies, and jazz groups also were spawned in the second half of the twentieth century, including the Alvin Ailey American Dance Theater, Steppenwolf Theatre Company, New York City Ballet, Lyric Opera of Chicago, and so on. (The same is true for many countries across the globe. Even when some of the major arts venues are older, the ensembles operating within them are young. The Royal Opera House, for example, was built in the mid-nineteenth century but the Royal Opera Company was formed in 1946.)

The burst of national pride, enthusiasm, and economic development that followed the war resulted in a remarkably fertile period of creativity in the United States. Working in that decade were the playwrights Tennessee Williams, Eugene O'Neill, and Arthur Miller; the composers Leonard Bernstein and Aaron Copland; the moviemakers Frank Capra and Alfred Hitchcock; the jazz artists Dizzy Gillespie, Duke Ellington, and Charlie Parker; and the choreographers Jerome Robbins, Agnes de Mille, and Martha Graham. We still revere the great movies, musicals, songs, novels, plays, and ballets that were created in that remarkable time.

And with the emergence of every important new artist, America's hunger for arts experiences only increased. Audiences were large, costs were relatively low, and the great and the good in each community were willing to underwrite the expenses that ticket sales could not cover.

This hunger for arts experiences was fed by television viewing. While those born after 1970 might not believe it, serious arts played a vital role in the development of commercial television. Many popular programs promoted the great opera singers, actors, and dancers of the time, including *The Bell Telephone Hour*, *Playhouse 90*, and *The Ed Sullivan Show*.

It is amazing to recall that Joan Sutherland was regularly featured in prime time on network television. Although an astonishing talent, Sutherland was not the most telegenic person; she would have been unlikely to get the bookings today. But a generation of Americans enjoyed Maria Callas, Isaac Stern, and Rudolph Nureyev, while many families huddled around their television sets to watch Leonard Bernstein conduct Young People's Concerts with the New York Philharmonic on CBS from 1958 until 1972! By contrast, the sole regularly scheduled network television program to feature classical music today is *The Kennedy Center Honors*, broadcast on one night each December and featuring only a short segment on the classical arts.

This appreciation for the arts was reflected in the lives of our leading politicians. President John F. Kennedy and his wife Jacqueline famously turned the White House into a salon where great artists and thinkers and writers could meet. When the Kennedys hosted the politically controversial cellist Pablo Casals in 1961, his performance made international news. The same was true of a gathering of Nobel Prize winners, of concerts by young artists, and other events.

As a result of the emergence of great talent and heightened visibility, the period from 1945 until 2000 saw an astonishing proliferation of arts organizations. And not just in New York, Chicago, and San Francisco. Important arts institutions were created in virtually every city and state in the Union, including Santa Fe, New Mexico; Cooperstown, New York; and Montgomery, Alabama. Today there are tens of thousands of arts organizations spread across the nation which attract many millions of visitors and inspire countless artists and audience members.

THE INCOME GAP

Another principal factor behind this artistic golden age was the willingness of an increasing number of people to support their local arts institutions, with financial contributions ranging from modest levels to much larger amounts. While it is true that, from the beginning of time, humans have had the twin needs to create and to be entertained, the history of arts organizations is entwined with the history of the people who are willing to pay for them. The visual and performing arts have never paid for themselves.

Why? Unlike most other industries, artists and arts institutions have never found a way to consistently boost worker productivity. In almost every other profitable industry, workers become more productive quarter after quarter. It now takes fewer person-hours to make a car or a blender—or to complete a banking transaction or send an oil invoice—than it did last year. This critical element affects every business; if workers get more productive, the cost of making the good or providing the service is less than it would be if worker productivity was flat.

Those of us in the arts, however, have a difficult time improving worker productivity. Musicians do not play Beethoven's Fifth Symphony faster every year, nor are any fewer dancers required to perform *Serenade* than when George Balanchine first created it in 1934. We do not ask sculptors to sculpt more quickly every year, nor do we ask composers to write a score in less time.

As a result, arts institutions suffer from a higher rate of inflation than the steel, automobile, or banking industries, where improvements in worker productivity lower one cost of production (total salaries) and offset, at least in part, inflation in other costs.

The fact that costs rise faster for arts organizations than for other industries is often misread as "artists don't handle money well" or "artists are wasteful." Many board members believe that if an arts organization were managed carefully, it would turn a profit. They cannot understand why an organization that makes something people like should run at a perpetual deficit.

This corporate prejudice can affect the way they govern their arts organization, encouraging them to try to cut budgets or to avoid addressing annual fund-raising requirements. Such board members start from the belief that arts managers are doing something wrong. They think that if corporate managers could run the arts organization, then it would become profitable, that if arts managers were smarter, fund-raising targets could be lower. They are simply wrong.

In truth, arts organizations are among the most efficient in the world, doing an immense amount of work with very small budgets. Even the largest arts organizations have modest budgets compared to ordinary corporations. And yet, many of the world's most important arts institutions have created huge brand awareness, with marketing commitments that are a small fraction of their less-well-known corporate counterparts. We have to be efficient because we serve so many masters: our board members, our audience, our donors, the press, and our peers.

To make matters more difficult, the opportunity for earned income in the arts comes with some built-in limitations. In many cases, the possible income for a given performance is limited by the number of seats in the theater. The Opera House at the Kennedy Center, for example, has 2,300 seats; that number has remained unchanged since it opened in 1971. Unlike most corporations, which can spread their costs over an ever-increasing customer base, each performance in this venue can serve only 2,300 patrons. Although our overheads grow quickly, our audience per show—and hence our real revenue for that show—is fixed.

When I was running the Alvin Ailey organization, I brought the dancers to perform at the Odeon of Herodes Atticus, a beautiful outdoor amphitheater built into the base of the Acropolis in Athens, Greece. It is one of the most amazing places in the world to experience a performance. The dancers were thrilled to perform on this ancient stage, with the Acropolis lit by the moon. I marveled, however, that the number of seats for the performances was the same as when the theater was built almost 2,000 years ago. There had been no opportunity for increases in real earned income, despite a huge increase in costs per performance!

Although arts institutions typically cannot increase the real earning potential for each performance, their costs rise quickly because

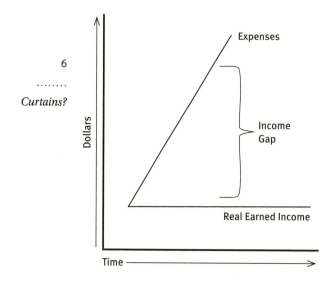

of the productivity problem. This causes an income gap that grows larger and larger every year. This economic dilemma has faced arts groups since the time of the construction of the Odeon of Herodes Atticus. When revenue growth is slower than expense growth, deficits are the result.

FILLING THE INCOME GAP

So what can we do to fill this income gap? One way to balance our budgets is to continue to raise ticket prices — as we have done for the past thirty years. But ticket prices have now grown so high that we have hit a point of diminishing returns: when going to the theater is too expensive, people stop going and revenue falls. Today, a pair of center orchestra tickets to the Metropolitan Opera cost $600! For just one performance! For that price, one could buy a computer and watch Leontyne Price and Luciano Pavarotti on YouTube for free, forever. High ticket prices do have an impact. After the Metropolitan Opera raised ticket prices 10 percent for the 2012–2013 season, ticket sales fell over $6 million, forcing management to reverse course. That season the Met earned only 69 percent of its potential ticket sales, down from the 90-percent range decades earlier.

The fact is that many people now believe the arts to be irrelevant to their lives. Because they have been priced out of the market, they have begun to look for other, less-expensive ways to be entertained. At the same time, advances in technology have provided many new and exciting ways to be entertained — and at almost no cost. While many arts institutions argue that they need to charge high prices to sustain themselves, they violate their own missions when ticket prices become so high as to discourage the audience for the art form they profess to be supporting. One can observe the impact of such pricing whenever a high-profile arts organization offers a free event. Just about everyone shows up for free concerts, operas, and dance performances: old and young, rich and poor, black and white. The arts are not unpopular — they have simply grown too expensive.

An alternative approach to filling the income gap has been to cut back on programming, either by doing less work or less ambitious work. A ballet company might do one less program each season; a theater company might do more small plays; an opera company might reduce the number of new productions, and so on. While this is a favored strategy of many board members — especially those who do not understand why costs rise and who believe that artists are wasteful — this is a losing proposition. Audiences and donors will not continue to support arts organizations that appear to do less and less. This should be one of the take-aways from the sad demise of the New York City Opera in 2013. When that company left Lincoln Center and became an itinerant ensemble, it also drastically reduced its number of productions each season. Although these productions received strong reviews, the performances were so diffuse in time and location that the organization could not maintain its family of audience members and donors.

Arts organizations must be frugal; we have nothing to spare and cannot justify wasting donors' contributions. But one simply cannot save one's way to health in the arts. A dollar cut from the budget can end up costing several dollars in lost ticket sales and contributions. It is possible to lower costs in productive ways, of course. When two ballet companies share a new production, for example, they both can appear vital to their constituents without either one bearing the full cost. Finding joint-venture partners for specific projects is a positive approach that continues to bring new work to our audiences. The exclusivity of a premier is often a selling point, but audience members could care less if the same production is shared with a city thousands of miles away.

A third key strategy for filling the income gap is to seek underwriting. Such patronage historically came from the church or from royalty. As these forms of support diminished by the end of nineteenth century, the burden of support was transferred to governments, both national and local. In the twentieth century, government support became central to the life and well-being of the arts sector. In France, one percent of the national budget is devoted to the arts; even in Saddam Hussein's Iraq, qualified artists were paid a monthly government stipend.

In those countries where government support grew to substantial levels, its easy availability had several important consequences. First, arts organizations could rely on a large infusion of cash each year; artists, therefore, could afford to think big. Not surprisingly, the largest concentration of world-famous arts organizations remains in Europe—where government support has been most plentiful. To this day, European arts organizations can mount huge productions, engage important artists, commission new works, and reap the benefits of worldwide visibility. It is difficult to imagine traveling to Moscow without visiting the Bolshoi, to Milan without a trip to La Scala, or to Madrid without a sojourn in the Prado. The fame, popularity, and economic contributions of these institutions have repaid the government investment in their activities several times over. Money does not always buy quality in the arts, but predictable grants allow artists and curators to pursue their own, personal visions—greatly increasing the chances of a special product.

Those arts organizations that received large government subsidies also could afford to be more adventuresome. Without the pressure to attract private donors—or earn large portions of their budgets from ticket sales—European arts organizations, in particular, could take big risks. They could push the envelope, comfortable in the knowledge that they would receive another large subsidy the following year—even if attendance was poor or the work presented was controversial. It is not surprising, for example, that *Regietheater*—in which a director takes the liberty of setting an opera in a time or place not intended by the composer—began in Europe. Although this innovative approach to opera production has made its way to the United States and other nations, it remains primarily identified with the European opera houses that could afford to take great risks.

While large state-supported arts organizations prospered in this environment, it was far harder for small and mid-size arts organizations to succeed. Government funds typically went only to a few, select organizations—the state opera, the state theater, and so on. Because a culture of private philanthropy had not yet been developed, it was more difficult for an independent arts organization to become established and grow. There were exceptions, of course. Over time, several important independent organizations were formed; these groups built an audience and gained such a reputation for excellence that they were eventually awarded state support. By the end of the twentieth century, some of these smaller organizations were receiving grants at the expense of the largest institutions.

In the United States, the reverse was true. Art and government have been separated since the nation's founding. (After all, the Puritans believed that music and dance were evil.) This situation forced private citizens who wanted the arts in their communities to provide the funds themselves. If funding had been left to local, state, or federal governments, there would be no San Francisco Opera, no Cleveland Orchestra, and no Oregon Shakespeare Festival. Although it is true that some state and local governments have invested quite heavily in the arts, apart from modest amounts granted by the National Endowment for the Arts, the National Endowment for the Humanities, and a few other agencies, federal arts support has been limited (not counting the indirect subsidy created by the tax deductibility of contributions to eligible not-for-profit organizations).

AMERICAN ARTS PHILANTHROPY

Unlike their European counterparts, American arts institutions developed with the support of individuals, corporations, and foundations. All of these donors wanted something in return for their gifts. For many, simple recognition was sufficient. Others desired access to artists, while some sought a modicum of control of the organizations they supported. The American-style arts board—with the expectation that members will "give, get, or get off"—was a major departure from the typical European board, appointed by the government to be the steward of public funds.

At the same time that American arts philanthropy was maturing, dynamic *for-profit* theater, recording, movie, radio, and television industries were developing concurrently. Over the course of the nineteenth and twentieth centuries, these industries grew very large, then were eclipsed by new technologies that presented and distributed entertainment in new ways. Although for-profit theater existed long before the twentieth century, for example, it flourished in the 1920s and beyond. The recording industry was born in 1877 with the invention of the phonograph. Early recordings featuring the great opera singers of the day sold relatively well, but the immense popularity of rock and roll transformed the business. The movie industry was born at the turn of the twentieth century then exploded with the advent of talking pictures in the 1920s. The rise of movies was followed closely by the development of radio, then the advent of television. In each case, new technology made art and entertainment easier to access and cheaper to enjoy. Often, it also made the experience of art more engaging for the audience.

And yet, through all of these developments, there remained a special place for not-for-profit arts organizations. Since early in the twentieth century, the U.S. tax code has provided a tax deduction for private contributions to charitable organizations and other not-for-profit ventures. In theory, this tax deduction was intended to encourage support for organizations that provide their communities with important services and products—services that for-profit entities would not undertake because of the lack of profit potential. In such cases, the costs were expected to be too high—or demand too low—to attract investment. Not-for-profit arts organizations, therefore, were not meant to duplicate the projects developed by for-profit entities; they were meant to be more adventuresome, to be of true service to the community, to provide educational opportunities, and to subsidize their ticket prices so that a broad spectrum of the public could partake. (High ticket prices are often cited by those who wish to limit or eliminate tax deductions for contributions to arts organizations; rather than supporting the public, the arts have become elitist, they claim, and therefore do not deserve even the indirect support of the government.)

Before the two world wars, arts sponsorship in the United States was dominated by a relatively small number of wealthy patrons. The Metropolitan Opera, for example, was founded in 1880 by twenty-two individuals who were unable to purchase boxes at the Academy of Music; to satisfy their desire for opera, they built a new theater and a new organization on their own. During the latter half of the twentieth century, however, the remarkable economic success of the educated classes left many more individuals and families with the resources to contribute—often very generously—to nascent arts organizations in their communities. Moreover, there was a prevailing sensibility that contributing to arts institutions— as well as medical, educational, and social-service organizations— was the responsibility of those who had enjoyed successful lives.

In Kansas City, Missouri, for example, donors backed a ballet company, several theater companies, an opera company, and a symphony, while also considerably expanding the local art museum. Several families of note—the Halls, the Kempers, the Nichols, and others—wanted to ensure that their city had the educational, medical, and artistic institutions that characterized all important cities. And Kansas City was not unique: similar investments were made in Indianapolis, Detroit, St. Louis, Atlanta, and other communities. America became a nation filled with young and vibrant arts organizations funded primarily by their audiences and by generous, local supporters.

In some countries, this new model was viewed with a curiosity tinged with scorn. Many believed that donors were controlling American art and that American artists were less free to create what they wanted. But no one could deny that everyday Americans were playing an active role in the development of arts institutions. These citizens voluntarily gave time and money in support of the organizations they loved—serving on boards and gala committees, contributing their own funds and encouraging others to give as well.

People found that contributing to the arts could be prestigious; many enjoyed the acclaim that accompanied a major gift to an institution, especially if that acclaim were somehow made permanent. Contributions for new buildings were particularly popular, for example, since these gifts were credited in public ways in perpetuity. The same was true for the contribution of objects to museum collections (or the funds to purchase those objects).

For many donors, access to famous artists was another, much appreciated perquisite of their contributions. It was interesting to meet these celebrated personalities—and something to brag about at the next several dinner parties.

And for those who wanted to enhance their position in society, arts patronage created a new kind of social standing. Opening-night performances, gala events, and special concerts provided opportunities to mingle with other leaders of the community. Corporations found that sponsoring arts events raised their profile, allowed their executives to make good contacts with other influential people, provided special benefits for their employees, and helped market their products. At a time when corporate earnings were growing—and a large share of corporate ownership resided close to headquarters—a sense of noblesse oblige motivated many executives to give generously.

Over time, a number of local and national foundations—such as the Ford Foundation and the Mellon Foundation—were formed to support a variety of causes, including the arts. In many instances, these foundations began by supporting organizations on the margins — artists of color or of the avant-garde. Such foundations recognized that a healthy arts ecology was a diverse one. In most communities, the majority of corporate and individual patrons supported the mainstream arts organizations. It was therefore left to other groups to ensure that the arts in America would not only be created by, and for, the prosperous.

Many people who gave to the arts, or to other not-for-profit organizations, did so not only for their own benefit but also for the sake of their offspring. In most American cities, people of means wanted to give their children the very best of everything. Education, sports, the arts, and the church were all considered essential to leading a good, full life. Children took piano lessons and ballet classes; they played Little League baseball and went to religious instruction. Liberal arts colleges were thriving, as were book and newspaper publishers, and a surprisingly large number of successful individuals felt it was essential that they regularly attend the symphony or theater. Attendance at these community events — the college or high school football game, the local symphony concerts, the weekly prayer service — was one of the responsibilities of a good citizen.

But it would be a mistake to suggest that philanthropy was the sole source of support for most arts organizations. In fact, the average contribution was small and the ranks of donors still relatively underdeveloped. For much of the twentieth century, ticket sales were the primary revenue source. In general, the costs of production were still low; few artists were unionized, for example, and touring was affordable. Most arts organization expected to earn between 50 and 70 percent of their budgets from ticket sales and tour fees.

THE SUBSCRIPTION MODEL

Many Americans do not appreciate that, until recently, subscriptions to the arts were a uniquely American phenomenon. To this day, subscriptions are not available in many countries of the world. The subscription model emerged from a combination of the patron's desire to attend with frequency and the organization's need to guarantee income. The practice of purchasing tickets for ten operas or concerts or plays a year, in advance, proved to be convenient for customers and a godsend for arts organizations.

For starters, a subscription purchase required only one transaction per year. (At a time when one could not purchase seats on-line, or even by telephone, this was truly a convenience.) It also guaranteed good seats and made performances easy to plan for. Attendance became part of one's social life; a subscriber expected to see the same people in the same seats on the same day of the week for years and years. It was comfortable and comforting.

The subscription model helped arts organizations in several ways. Arts organizations typically suffer from huge swings in cash flow. They are cash-poor when creating new productions—building sets and costumes and rehearsing the cast, for example—and cash-rich after performances have begun and tickets have been sold. Cash was typically tightest during the summer and early autumn months, when few performances were held. By selling subscriptions for the following season in late spring, however, arts organizations gained access to money when they needed it most—when rehearsals were beginning, but before the majority of single tickets were sold. This advance of funds was critical to sustaining the cash flow of most arts organizations.

Subscriptions also allowed the artistic leadership to become more adventuresome. Most customers were willing to accept a subscription as long as a few of the performances were of well-known works or featured important artists. This was true even if some performances in the series were less familiar. This provided a measure of artistic freedom, since organizations could sponsor new or unfamiliar works or engage less well-known performers to accompany the selection of surefire hits. In fact, the subscription model facilitated the creation of many of the then-new works of art we enjoy to this day.

Subscriptions could reduce costs as well, as it was far cheaper to market a subscription for six or eight performances than to market each performance separately. In the days before e-mail, the cost of a subscription brochure, in addition to a follow-up telephone call or reminder postcard, could be spread over the sale of multiple tickets. Sales of single tickets, on the other hand, required individual newspaper advertisements, direct mail pieces, and other expensive marketing vehicles. Unsurprisingly, a seminal arts marketing text, by Danny Newman, was entitled *Subscribe Now!*

The analogous model for museums was membership. By purchasing a membership, people could visit the museum several times for one fixed cost, while the museum got the admission fees up front, before the costs of mounting the next exhibition were incurred.

Over time, subscriptions and memberships powered the growth of thousands of arts organizations. (In those days of relatively inexpensive tickets, it was not a challenge for many customers to buy a full series.) At the peak of this phenomenon, some 60 or 70 percent of the tickets available for a major arts institution might have been sold by subscription. Eventually, however, a successful arts organization would run out of seats to sell. The theater would be full. And yet costs kept rising and artists' dreams continued to develop.

As arts budgets continued to grow, while ticket revenue was capped, the need for additional income became apparent. (Like any not-for-profit organization, an arts organization continues to grow until it becomes difficult to find enough resources to fund that growth.) Unfortunately for most arts organizations, however, the contributions of their initial supporters could take them only so far. Time and resources would eventually become exhausted, or donors turned their attentions elsewhere. The Metropolitan Opera, for example, far outgrew its original twenty-two founders; today, a huge network of donors is required to support the annual budget. To grow and develop, arts organizations had to raise ticket prices. But they also had to expand their roster of contributors—which meant they began to compete with other arts institutions for donors' attention.

Thankfully, the number of individuals with resources to contribute, the number of corporations who believed that supporting the arts was part of their civic duty, and the number of foundations established to support philanthropic endeavors all increased as the need for funding increased. While some arts organizations did not learn how to compete successfully in this environment, many others grew to become important both to their communities and to their art forms. The number of arts organizations in the United States with annual budgets exceeding $1 million is now huge.

DIVERSITY AND THE ARTS

Until the 1960s, the vast majority of American arts organizations were Eurocentric, serving middle- and upper-class white patrons. After a number of high-profile debuts with mainstream arts organizations—Marian Anderson's debut at the Metropolitan Opera in 1955 was the artistic equivalent of Jackie Robinson's engagement by the Brooklyn Dodgers—artists of color (with the support of major foundations and local government agencies) were encouraged to create institutions to serve their own communities. Although some of these organizations, like the Alvin Ailey American Dance Theater, were formed in the late 1950s, the majority were created after the 1968 assassination of Dr. Martin Luther King, Jr. In the years that followed, the artistic landscape was no longer all white, as cities like Denver, Philadelphia, and Dallas established African American, Latino, and Asian American theater and dance companies, museums, and musical ensembles.

Theaters of color were particularly prominent and inventive. While there were black theater productions as early as the 1820s, the development of African American theater *companies* really exploded around 1960. In 1959, *A Raisin in the Sun* was the first original Broadway production to be written by an African American playwright (Lorraine Hansberry) and led by an African American director (Lloyd Richards). In the years that followed, dozens of theater companies of color—from Penumbra Theatre in St. Paul, Minnesota, to Teatro Visión in San Jose, California, to Crossroads Theater in New Brunswick, New Jersey—created important works that reflected the concerns of their constituents.

At the same time, a group of pioneering dance-makers also started vibrant organizations—Joan Myers Brown, Arthur Mitchell, Tina Ramirez, and H. T. Chen, among them—that gave homes to dancers, choreographers, and designers of color. None of these theater or dance companies had an easy time sustaining themselves. Their base audiences could neither afford expensive tickets nor make major contributions. Arts organizations of color relied primarily on grants from foundations and government agencies. While these grants were vitally necessary, they also allowed the organizations to grow without creating the broad base of individual donors or potent board of directors that typically forms the bedrock of support for their mainstream counterparts. This would become a problem when the organizations grew so large that a few government and foundation grants were not sufficient to support them, especially when government funding began to decline.

A COMPLICATED AND WONDERFUL QUILT

At the same time that new and diverse arts organizations were forming, some arts patrons became concerned that the full range of the arts were not accessible enough to those without the means to pay for expensive tickets. As a result, new organizations were formed to bring the underserved—including children, minorities, people with disabilities, rural citizens, and those in difficult urban settings—into both the arts and the audience.

To provide support for arts groups themselves, a number of service organizations also were formed, including the American Alliance of Museums, Opera America, Dance USA, League of American Orchestras, and Theater Communications Group, among others. Added to this mix were advocacy groups such as Americans for the Arts, groups that supported American artists abroad, and so on.

Accompanying the development of this broad range of producing, presenting, and service organizations was an equally wide range of music, theater, and dance conservatories and arts schools, along with a growing number of arts management programs. In the decades after 1960, a large, complicated quilt of arts organizations blanketed the nation. While it is true that not every citizen was served equally, almost anyone interested in the arts—from Alaska to Key West—could access them if they tried.

What is both fascinating and crucial to observe about this same period, however, is that the distribution model for the arts did not substantially change. Under this model, arts organizations produced live performances and exhibitions. Those with an interest in these programs—and the means to pay for them—left their homes, traveled to the appropriate venues, and watched a performance or viewed an exhibition at the prescribed time. (That is not to imply that the product line of arts organizations did not expand. During the last quarter of the twentieth century, many arts organizations also produced programs aimed at building new audiences; training young artists, curators, and administrators; and meeting the educational needs of adult audience members.) But the fundamental products—performances of theater, music, and dance, and exhibitions of art—remained much the same as they did in the nineteenth century, even though other forms of entertainment and distribution were changing radically.

America in the 1990s was not the same as America in the 1950s. Government budgets were devoted increasingly to the costs of the military and various entitlement programs; the resources available for arts education were diminished. In fact, some of the expansion in arts programming mentioned earlier was intended to replace public-school educational programs that were already on the wane.

Today we have a generation of college students who did not routinely receive arts programming in elementary and high school—a generation that is, by and large, culturally illiterate with respect to classical repertory. Even some of the best-educated people born after 1980 have difficulty identifying an opera by Mozart, a ballet by Balanchine, or a play by Oscar Wilde. This is true even though arts organizations continued to mount exhibitions and performances.

Of the thousands of arts ventures that began life in the 1950s, '60s, and '70s, many ceased operating when it became too difficult to maintain an audience or find the necessary resources. A large number, however, became mid-sized or larger. And the larger they grew, the more money they needed. To win a wider audience and more funds, many organizations expanded their geographic scope. What was originally a rather quaint cottage industry today contributes more to the national economy than tourism!

America's twentieth-century growth in arts activities was accompanied by a building boom. Theaters, concert halls, and museums were erected all over the United States. By the 1960s, the notion of an arts center—a campus that could house a multitude of arts organizations—was becoming popular. New York built its Lincoln Center, Washington its Kennedy Center. Today, there are arts centers in numerous American cities, from Costa Mesa, California, to Miami, Florida. Construction costs were relatively easy to fund, as naming an arts center (or a portion of it) became a way for the wealthy to assure that posterity would appreciate their contributions. (Unfortunately, it was easier to raise money for the buildings themselves than for operating those buildings, but that did not seem to matter either to donors or to city planners.)

The growth in the arts also spurred the development of unions for musicians, dancers, and actors. These unions, naturally, pressed for more work for their members. To accommodate these demands, some ballet companies developed seasons of thirty-six weeks or more, while many symphonies became year-round employers of their musicians. This placed increased pressure on boards and administrators to find both more resources and more performing opportunities. In many cities, the number of symphony or ballet performances exceeded demand, particularly as the younger generation was finding its entertainment in new and different ways.

Such pressures had less effect on museums. Because museums typically do not recreate their art every day, once an exhibition is hung, the marginal costs of opening an extra week or two are small. For all arts institutions, however, the development of unions meant higher salaries and more costly benefits.

As overall costs increased, many organizations decided to add professional staff. After all, if one needed to sell more tickets, then one needed a larger and more sophisticated marketing staff. And if an organization needed to raise more funds, then it needed a more robust development staff. The complaint began to emerge that administrators were overshadowing artists. Increasingly, decisions about repertory were made to please donors and to attract larger audiences. This introduced a tension between artists and

management that often resulted in the production of less interesting art.

In the last two decades of the twentieth century, artists increasingly behaved like naughty children ("I want this" or "I want that")
and administrators like angry parents ("No, we can't afford it").
In response, some artists began to plan to a budget rather than
to dream, allowing the limit on funds to limit their imaginations.
From one American city to another, repertory seasons began to
look more alike, and art began to look more alike.

This was less true in Europe and elsewhere. With governments
providing large subsidies, there was no need to woo new donors
every year. By the end of the century, however, government subsidies were falling and even European arts organizations were
struggling to build private philanthropy while maintaining artistic
independence.

The increasing mobility of artists themselves added to a conver-
gence in arts programming across the globe. There were Russian
dancers at American Ballet Theatre and American dancers at the
Bolshoi. And it was not uncommon to see works by Balanchine,
Robbins, Wheeldon, and Ratmansky whether one lived in New
York, London, St. Petersburg, or San Francisco!

Despite all of these concerns, the arts industry continued to grow.
The largest arts organizations in the United States now had budgets
of several hundred million dollars a year. There was a major dance
company in Boise, Idaho, an opera company in Cooperstown, New
York, and symphonies in literally hundreds of cities across the nation. A seemingly endless supply of private donors had been willing
to ratchet up their giving. And a million-dollar contribution to an
arts organizations might not even be mentioned in the press.

The largesse of donors hid the fact that the arts industry had become less and less able to earn its own way. Ambition—combined
with the productivity gap—worked to increase budgets faster than
either audiences or donors could pay for them. The conventional
wisdom was that "All arts organizations have deficits." And in any
case, what harm was there in borrowing from an endowment to pay
current shortfalls? Wasn't that what endowments were for?

By the turn of the century, Americans were enjoying a surfeit of excellent art at home, along with a bounty of touring programs and exhibits. In major U.S. cities, it was not uncommon to be able to see the Bolshoi Ballet, the London Symphony Orchestra, and the Peking Opera in a single season. Budgets were high, arts venues were beautiful, donors were happy, boards were proud.

We were indeed blessed.

America the Beautiful

TO HAVE AND HAVE NOT

. . . .

THE ARTS IN THE TWENTY-FIRST

. . . .

CENTURY (TO DATE)

And then came (in no particular order): economic instability, the Internet explosion, the death of the recording industry, the near-death of subscriptions, the renewed focus on STEM (science, technology, engineering, and math) and resulting swoon in the liberal arts, the introduction of movie-theater opera, the erosion of newspaper readership and its threat to serious arts criticism, the aging of the donor base, the raiding of endowments, and the search for "new models."

Although many of these trends have roots in the past thirty years, each continues to cause fundamental shifts in the arts ecology. The first years of the twenty-first century have seen unparalleled threats to the quality, quantity, and diversity of the arts. We can no longer take access to the arts for granted. In one brief period, we witnessed the closure of the New York City Opera, a year-long lock out of the Minnesota Orchestra, and strikes by the San Francisco Symphony and the Chicago Symphony Orchestra. The Penumbra Theater in St. Paul, Minnesota, had to suspend its operations, while the Miami City Ballet faced closure, and so on and so on.

How did these disasters happen?

DECLINING SUBSCRIPTIONS

The subscription model was based on the desire of audience members to attend performances frequently, with a high degree of regularity and predictability. For it to work, subscribers had to want to go to the opera every Thursday or the ballet on alternate Saturdays. In the 1950s and 1960s, people led far more regular lives, with far less business travel, than they do today. (Ironically, active and successful businesspeople today travel more even as innovations in communications technology, like videoconferencing, have made it easier to do business without traveling.) In those years, women made the majority of arts-purchase decisions for their families, and often did not work outside the home. As more and more women have assumed executive positions, the ability to predict a family's regular availability for arts performances has been severely hampered.

Subscription sales also fell as ticket prices increased. When a five-performance subscription cost only $100, many people felt they could afford this sum to support their local theater company or symphony. When this amount tripled, quadrupled, or more, far fewer people were willing to send a check well in advance of the season.

Since the 1970s, therefore, we have seen a steady erosion of subscription sales. This has placed tremendous pressure on arts organizations, reducing the funds available at the beginning of a season (or before), and creating cash-flow problems at the very time when revenue is at its lowest point.

The loss of subscription sales also increased marketing costs for almost every arts organization. It is more expensive, and takes more staff time, to sell tickets to four separate events than to sell one ticket for a series of four productions. The cost of programmatic marketing—marketing to ticket buyers—has increased dramatically as the number of subscribers has fallen. Large single-ticket marketing campaigns require more campaign materials as well as a larger number of marketing staff.

In the absence of subscriptions, organizations could no longer count on the most famous and accessible works—*Swan Lake*, Beethoven's Ninth Symphony, and so on—or the most celebrated artists—such as Placido Domingo or Yo-Yo Ma—to help bolster sales for less well known fare and newer artists. In past years, 50 or 60 percent of the house might already be sold by the end of a subscription campaign. Now, every performance must be sold on its own merits. As a result, works that are new or different—or difficult to describe—are scarier to produce.

Under these changed conditions, marketing departments now have much "advice" for programmers. After all, too much Berg and not enough Tchaikovsky can kill the bottom line. Why not engage a television star to perform that role? And can you produce a work that will attract a younger audience? A richer one?

Fund-raisers have their own concerns, weighing in with the artistic preferences of key donors. If the donors are unhappy, the not-so-veiled threat goes, then the organization could be in danger of insolvency. Because the fund-raising department typically has the ear of board members, their concerns often have substantial ramifications. As money gets tighter, board members typically start to exert more authority over programming; what began as a suggestion can become a demand.

With the increased influence of marketers, fund-raisers, and board members, programming can become less adventuresome. And while this might mean higher average ticket sales or happier current donors, it also means that the outlier—the new and different work that captures the imagination in astonishing ways—is less likely to be created and presented.

And it is these very works that build new audiences for the arts, inspiring new donors and propelling existing ones to increase their giving and become more involved in the life of the organization. When a truly astonishing new work is introduced, audiences flock to see it—both traditional audiences and new ones. Innovative works remind people why they care about the arts in the first place. These are the works that get people talking about an arts organization, that make it impossible to ignore an arts institution, that make it sexy to participate—as a donor, board member, volunteer, or audience member. With fewer of these projects in development, the arts have lost a major magnet for support.

To be sure, many arts institutions still sell subscriptions and still have subscribers. Many older, wealthier patrons continue to value the convenience of subscribing, and those who have retired generally have more flexible schedules. Marketers, for their part, are well aware of the implications of lost subscriptions, and have tried desperately to find new mechanisms to build subscriber rolls. Some organizations now offer flexible subscriptions, for example, which allow audience members to exchange tickets for a more convenient performance. Other incentives include discounts, free food or drink, special performances, lecture series, and even gifts.

By and large, however, subscribers now comprise only about 20 percent of current ticket buyers, compared with the 60 or 70 percent that arts organizations might have expected thirty years ago. As a result, the excitement, innovativeness, and financial health of the arts have all suffered.

THE RISE OF NEW TECHNOLOGIES

At the same time that the subscription model was ailing, new technologies were in development. Those of us born in the 1950s cannot remember a world without computers. In our youngest days, we watched a Sperry Univac match couples — many of whom later married — on Art Linkletter's television show. But computers were so large and expensive that we did not ever expect them to be as prevalent in our lives as radios and televisions. Computers were for big corporations, for the military, and for other government agencies. Although we felt vaguely threatened that computers would do us out of our jobs, we had no notion that they would invade our homes.

Over the past sixty years, of course, computers have become far smaller, far more powerful, and remarkably less expensive. (As it turns out, the invention of the transistor was, perhaps, the most important invention since the wheel.) Computers have enhanced our lives — and played havoc with them. It is difficult to think of one aspect of our existence that has not been influenced, in some way, by the introduction of computer technology. For many young people, a smartphone or tablet accompanies every waking hour. (They might take a break for the gym, but would still listen to their iPods as they worked out.) Asking our children to forego electronics is the equivalent of asking our generation to go without electricity.

Computers have had a huge impact on the way arts events are produced and marketed. While the loss of subscription revenue has increased the costs of programmatic marketing, computer technology helped minimize the damage.

Historically, the arts were marketed by direct mail, through bro-chures sent to the home, by posters in public places, by advertise-ments placed in newspapers and magazines, and, less frequently, by radio and television ads. These means of advertising all en-courage brevity of message and a standardized, untailored appeal. A poster or newspaper advertisement often featured little more than the name of the work, the major artists involved, the perfor-mance dates, and a telephone number to call. And television and radio commercials remain so expensive that they must be kept very short. Direct mail pieces could contain more information but were also less dynamic.

This meant that arts marketers could not adjust their messages to meet the needs of different kinds of consumers, nor could they put much information about artistic content or critical response in any one advertisement. This made it difficult to promote perfor-mances and exhibitions. Instead, of reaching potential ticket buy-ers with a message tailored especially for them, one had to repeat the same generic message, hoping that the customer eventually would be convinced to buy.

The task could be especially challenging for new or esoteric pro-grams, since the marketer could not provide much information about the nature of the work and what made it compelling, or why the less well known artist was worthy of such exposure. To con-vey this much information in a newspaper advertisement or radio commercial would have been incredibly expensive. Such concerns were less of an issue when so many tickets were sold on subscrip-tion, but as subscription sales dwindled, marketing new work be-came far more problematic.

Now that the Internet is accessible almost everywhere—and vir-tually every potential ticket buyer owns at least one computer de-vice—arts marketers have the ability to deliver a great deal more information at virtually no cost, and to tailor each message to the particular recipient. Web sites and e-mail blasts can now include video or audio clips, photographs, biographies of artists, endorse-ments from critics, and so on. Those who care specifically about a certain repertory, individual artist, or particular price level can be reached with different messages. The activities of marketing departments are now limited only by their imaginations and their databases. A student of mine from Ethiopia told me that while his audience did not have computers, they did have cell phones; he marketed exclusively through text messages!

To further refine their messages, arts marketers can now collect a remarkable amount of information from everyone who purchases a ticket: what types of performances they enjoy, which performance days or times are most attractive to them, which artists or performers or composers or choreographers they like most, how far they live from the theater, and on and on.

This is a vast change from previous decades, when very little data was available and all of it had to be tabulated by hand. We used to be happy to receive weekly updates; now we have real-time sales reports that tell us what's selling from minute to minute. To verify box-office reports, we used to sit and count ticket stubs; now we can monitor who actually came to the theater through bar-code scans.

When used carefully and creatively, data helps target specific customers with specific messages. This is becoming particularly important as the number of arts organizations that send e-mails increases; one wants to be sure that recipients are willing to open and read your e-mails because they trust it contains a message that is relevant to them. In the past, arts organizations competed for visibility only with others that could afford to mail brochures and buy advertising. Now that cost is no longer a barrier, people can become inundated with marketing messages. And for many consumers, it is difficult to discern the relative quality of various offerings simply from the contents of an e-mail. In Washington, D.C., for example, there are often as many as four different *Nutcracker* productions in December. But are the "Stars of Russian Ballet" truly stars? And is Moscow Ballet Theatre the same as Moscow City Ballet or Ballet Moscow?

Web sites also offer a great deal of information to potential ticket buyers. The number of Web sites available is now so vast, however, that getting someone to pay attention to yours has become a major challenge. Simply printing a Web address on letters, e-mails, mugs, and t-shirts is not enough; we have become so used to seeing such addresses that they hardly register anymore. There has to be a compelling reason to visit a Web site; it must be interesting, engaging, helpful, enlightening, or entertaining.

More importantly, there has to be a compelling reason to *return* to a Web site. Organizations with less to sell are at a distinct disadvantage here, since the information on their sites changes less often. When someone visits a site two or three times and sees the exact same information, they will probably not visit again.

In general, the arts organizations with the best name recognition and the most to offer are the ones that are getting people to view their Web sites and open their e-mails. The Kennedy Center, for example, presents 2,000 performances a year; the information on its site changes every few seconds. As a result, a small arts organization that offers four shows a year will have difficulty competing for their share of the online audience. This is only one reason why the separation between the "haves" and the "have-nots" is beginning to increase. The larger, more visible organizations not only have more drawing power, they also can invest more in their sites, filling them with attractive and engaging content.

While Internet technologies have been a boon to arts marketers, they also have introduced a host of new entertainment offerings. These offerings compete for the hearts and minds of both potential customers and donors, and are proving increasingly difficult for arts institutions to overcome.

In the 1950s, people could entertain themselves with the radio, movies, books, and arts experiences, along with three television networks. Today, there are literally hundreds of television channels, and more opportunities to be entertained on the Internet than one can easily count. YouTube alone provides access to hundreds of thousands of performances of all types. Because we can communicate far more freely and inexpensively than in the past, people also spend free time sending and reading e-mails, tweets, and Facebook postings. They develop Pinterest pages and upload their photographs to Instagram. They play video games like Angry Birds and Candy Crush. And a few still read books and listen to music!

The fact that ticket prices for live performances have grown so high only highlights the stark differences among the choices facing arts consumers today. Why pay to go to the local opera company when one can hear the greatest opera singers perform for free? And the price of the ticket is just one cost of attending a live performance; there are often parking, food, and babysitting expenses as well. Wouldn't it be easier — and far, far cheaper — to stay at home and watch a few YouTube videos, then play a little Candy Crush while monitoring your Facebook page and sending e-mails?

The fact that all of this can be done on one's own schedule is especially attractive. People no longer have to be at the concert hall at 8:00 p.m. They can watch whatever they want, whenever they want. This desire for independence has had a substantial impact even on television-viewing habits. One no longer needs to watch a favorite show only when it is broadcast. Now one can record that show and see it later, or watch via streaming services like Hulu and Netflix. Many people now binge-watch, viewing an entire series at a sitting, one episode after the other.

While binge-watching has become a trend, it also represents an exception to another trend. More people are now listening only to individual parts of albums, or viewing only particular scenes of movies and performances. As a result, posting an entire performance online no longer satisfies the audience. Because so many people only want to watch an excerpt or two, it is essential to divide performances into tracks, so that specific highlights can be easily identified, accessed, and shared on Twitter or Facebook.

The desire for "bite-sized" experiences has been developing for decades. It started perhaps with *USA Today*, the newspaper that reduced major news stories to a few paragraphs. Since its introduction in 1982, many people have been more happy to read a short news blurb than a lengthy and detailed story. Twitter is a natural outgrowth of this trend. People enjoy reading 140-character messages from a favorite actor, sports star, or musician. Rather than feeling superficial, it feels current and honest and real. The fact that so many people are tweeting inappropriate or impolitic statements only enhances the feeling that this is a more open mode of communication than the lengthy, edited interview in a glossy magazine.

This trend works against the viewing of full-length plays and operas, many of which extend past four hours in duration. For a society that is content with headlines, a single aria on YouTube is now sufficient. Not surprisingly, many opera companies have turned to abridged versions; the Metropolitan Opera, for example, has created a shortened version of *The Magic Flute*, directed by Julie Taymor, that runs for less than two hours. While it is marketed to children and families, many childless adults prefer this shorter version as well.

Twitter and other forms of social networking have been a mixed blessing for arts marketers. While it is cheap, easy, and fast to send a tweet (or six or ten), such messages cannot be very long, complicated, or deep. Like the newspaper advertisements of the last century, one is limited to a brief, often superficial message. Just try to explain the plot of a new opera, or the pedigree of a foreign choreographer, on a tweet. The information will be sketchy and the subtleties lost. Not to mention the difficulty of getting people to follow the tweets of an arts organization when 400 million other tweets are sent each day.

As technology has changed how and what we watch, it also has affected the experience of *watching* itself. Audience members traditionally expected to come to a theater, sit in the dark, and witness a performance. Today's audiences, however—especially the younger ones—value *participating* in the performance as well. While a few shows have featured audience participation in the past— *The Mystery of Edwin Drood*, a musical based on the Dickens novel, famously asked the audience to vote for the show's ending, including the name of the murderer—the visual and performing arts were not typically thought of as participatory. One went to a museum or performance to admire the work of great artists—not to participate in the work oneself.

But new communications capabilities have fostered a desire to play a more active role while being entertained. From voting for one's favorite singer on *American Idol* to playing fantasy football, we have become far less apt to merely sit back and watch. This works against most of the classical arts, of course, making it even more challenging to attract new and younger audiences. Some organizations have tried, with modest success, to invite audience participation, but the Bruch Violin Concerto has so far defied this trend.

ECONOMIC INSTABILITY IN THE TWENTY-FIRST CENTURY

All of the changes mentioned thus far have been occurring at a time of great economic uncertainty. Given the collapse of the tech bubble, the aftereffects of 9/11, the 2008 mortgage crisis, the bankruptcy of Lehman Brothers, and the ensuing recession, the first ten years of this century have not been calm. While stocks regained their value by 2013, employment and income were still lagging and many individuals, corporations, and communities were adversely affected.

During each of these shocks to the economy, the arts took a battering. In fact, every source of income for arts organizations was affected in a dramatic way. Government funding diminished substantially, especially at the state and local levels, as the economic downturn emboldened those who believe that government deficits were the root cause of the instability. The search for ways to trim budgets led inevitably (though without much impact on deficits) to cutting arts support. Local government support for the arts fell 18 percent between 2008 and 2012, while state funding fell 27 percent in the same period. In inflation-adjusted dollars, total government funding for the arts (federal, state, and local) fell a staggering 31 percent between 1992 and 2012!

Because foundations rely on the returns from their investment portfolios, foundation grants suffered as stocks and bonds plummeted in value during much of the past decade. And since many foundations had made multi-year commitments to their grantees, their ability to fund new projects was severely hampered during and immediately following the recession. Many foundations used this period to evaluate their core missions and to assess standards for the organizations they would continue to support. In many cases, arts organizations must now demonstrate a far higher degree of fiscal responsibility to qualify for foundation support than in the past. While this is undoubtedly an appropriate requirement, it has inevitably created pressure on smaller arts organizations with less potent boards and more modest fund-raising and marketing capabilities. Ironically, many foundations also have begun to place greater emphasis on the capitalization of arts organizations, with many grants going toward working capital reserves and endowments. When grants are devoted to such vehicles instead of other expenses—such as art-making, marketing, fund-raising, and financial management—it becomes far more difficult for arts institutions to show the operating results that qualify them for a grant in the first place!

Unsurprisingly, corporate giving also fell during this turbulent period. As shares lost value (sometimes in large increments), shareholders made it more difficult for corporations to justify donations to the arts. While some funding could be justified on the basis of marketing efforts, many corporations drastically reduced—or even eliminated—their support for the arts. Those corporations that maintained their support typically underwrote programming at organizations with higher levels of visibility. It was these organizations that provided corporations with the best return on their arts "investments." While corporations used to give in order to be considered good citizens, they now can justify arts sponsorships only when they provide measurable returns.

This change occurred in part because of the changing nature of corporate ownership. While the stock market has always allowed non-locals to purchase shares, corporate ownership has become far more dispersed than in the past, with many U.S.-based companies now owned by foreign investors or international corporations. This reduces the likelihood that a business will feel loyalty to the community in which it operates. Arts organizations in Hartford, Connecticut, for example, which once boasted a number of insurance-company headquarters, now must rely on executives living thousands of miles away to decide on sponsorships. This makes it far harder for arts executives to build strong relationships with decision-makers and to make them aware of the impact of their contributions.

Individuals typically are the most loyal of donors; a higher proportion of individual donors maintain support for an arts organization for an extended period of time than corporate or foundation donors. With the onset of recession, however, individuals with falling incomes were forced to eliminate some of their giving or could no longer afford to give to the arts at all. And the length and depth of this recession, with its associated high levels of unemployment, were particularly unusual—affecting arts giving more than other recessions of recent memory.

This recession most affected the giving capacity of those with the least to give. While many affluent people lost a portion of their wealth, most still had enough discretionary income to contribute something to the not-for-profit organizations of their choice. Those with limited means, however, were left with nothing extra. As a result, arts organizations that served people of color, rural residents, and inner-city communities all suffered disproportionately during the economic downturn. Some individuals who retained the means to give to the arts used the recession as a ready excuse for paring away those organizations that were no longer of real interest. Such donors might maintain support for the organizations to which they felt closest, but end their support for marginal groups.

For similar reasons, the reduction in individual giving was matched by a reduction in demand for arts events. The same people who cut their donations because of reduced earnings also purchased fewer subscriptions and fewer single tickets. For many, the freely available online forms of entertainment became easy substitutes for expensive performances. This made it especially difficult for organizations that could not afford major productions or expensive marketing campaigns (or produced less well known and less accessible work) to maintain ticket sales.

What types of organizations suffered most during these times? Those most reliant on government and foundation grants—since these sources of funds fell the most. Not surprisingly, the arts groups that rely more on these grants, in terms of percentage of contributed revenue, are rural organizations, avant-garde organizations, service organizations, and organizations of color. As corporations made difficult decisions about which organizations to fund, these same smaller groups were the first to be cut—since they produced the least visibility for corporate donors. And while these organizations relied less on individual donors, it was their individual donors who were most affected by the recession and most likely to cut arts giving. As these groups became sicker and sicker, they competed even less well with larger arts organizations than before.

When the smaller arts organizations, the ones on the margins, begin to suffer—while the largest organizations become increasingly potent—our entire arts quilt begins to unravel. We lose the new artists who bring fresh vision and insight. We lose the institutions that attract new audiences to the arts. We lose the projects that bring vitality to the arts community. We lose the organizations that push art forms to change and grow. And we become less competitive with other forms of entertainment that embrace and nurture new technologies, new artists, new ideas.

Thankfully, not every such organization was forced to endure reduced levels of revenue during the early part of the current century. Those organizations—both large and small—with strong artistic products, sophisticated marketing and fund-raising operations, and strong governing boards were able to weather the storm.

The organizations that had the most success during this difficult period were those that had the flexibility to adjust programming and reduce expenses. Some theater, opera, and ballet companies staged smaller works, works already in the repertory, or works more familiar to the audience. While this is certainly not a long-term prescription for success in the arts, it was an effective short-term approach for surviving an economic decline.

The hardest-hit organizations were those with the least flexibility. Symphony orchestras, for example, essentially pay the same number of musicians every week. They can save on a guest conductor or soloist, but doing so typically is a losing strategy at the box office. It was not surprising, therefore, to see so many orchestras in disarray—going bankrupt, proposing massive cuts in player salaries, and so on. We are likely to see far more of these situations as boards and management look for ways to cut costs in the face of declining subscriptions and single-ticket sales, reduced levels of contributions, competition from new forms of entertainment, reduced attention by mainstream media, and the growing perception that symphony orchestras are old-fashioned and irrelevant.

The Minnesota Orchestra, one of the most admired ensembles in the nation, endured a lock-out of over one year. In the dispute, board and staff members believed they could not develop a credible strategy for balancing the budget without huge reductions in the salaries of musicians. The musicians resisted this proposal, believing that the organization had not been smart about building its audience and donor base. Members of the community split their support, with many corporate leaders encouraging the board to hold firm, and many music lovers lobbying in favor of the musicians.

That this issue developed in a major Midwest city is also no surprise. While the entire nation has been gripped by recession and instability, the Midwestern portion of the United States has been hardest hit by another phenomenon—a major shift in where and how manufactured products are made. Manufacturing employment hit its peak in the United States in 1979, when 19.4 million workers were employed by this sector. By 2010, this number had fallen to 11.5 million!

In an effort to improve productivity, many products are now produced largely by machines—which are far less costly than people. And those products still being assembled by people are primarily being made offshore, in countries with far lower salary costs. This has reduced the demand for manufacturing labor in the United States, particularly in the so-called Rust Belt, a region that played an outsized role in U.S. manufacturing activity earlier in the twentieth century. The drastic reduction in manufacturing employment caused significant changes in a part of the nation that has relied for generations on well-paying union jobs. Unionized manufacturing jobs provided a comfortable lifestyle for millions of Americans. While these employees were relatively well paid, however, they were typically undereducated and ill-prepared to shift careers as manufacturing activity dwindled. People who had worked in large factories could not easily transition to high-technology jobs. Many were forced to accept service-sector positions instead, which paid far less than their previous jobs, if they could find jobs at all.

In addition to affecting the earned income of both individuals and organizations, the economic challenges of this century also posed problems for endowment income. Endowments are meant to be preserved in perpetuity. While any income on these funds can be spent, the principal amounts are not meant to be touched. A typical arts organization "takes" about 5 percent of its endowment's value every year as income — if, that is, it is lucky enough to have an endowment.

Endowment income has been venerated for being "guaranteed." Board members of many arts institutions often believe "All we need is an endowment." And it is certainly better to have a large endowment fund than not to have one. But we have learned in this century that endowment income is not guaranteed at all. After the stock market dives of 2001 and 2008, institutions that depended on their endowments were dramatically affected, suffering losses both in the value of principal and the percentage available for income. Since most such institutions use a rolling average of the last three years of returns when calculating endowment income, the impact of endowment losses stay with an organization for several years. Those institutions with the largest endowments — typically museums and orchestras — were hurt the most by the stock market dips. (Of all not-for-profit organizations, universities were hit the hardest by far — more than seventy had endowments that exceeded a billion dollars of principal!)

Taken together, the various economic problems faced by arts organizations in the past decade have been cataclysmic in their effect. But it would be wrong to blame all the problems faced by the arts on the economy, as many observers have done. Rather than causing all of our problems, the downturns merely *revealed* problems that had been lying beneath the surface for many years, including an over-reliance on a few donors, an inadequate growth in earned income, and the presence of weak governing boards.

NEW OPPORTUNITIES FOR THE ARTS

Some arts organizations have responded to the underlying shifts in demand for the arts in innovative ways. We now have concerts with video and other media, shorter performances, more convenient times, flexible purchase plans, even tweeted orchestras (in which the conductor tweets throughout the performance).

One of the most innovative approaches has been the broadcast of live performances to movie theaters and other venues. This helps to ease one of the most profound economic problems facing the arts—the inability to increase revenue per theater seat. (See "The Income Gap" in chapter 1.) By selling seats in remote locations, arts organizations can raise their earned income beyond the value of the seats in the theater in which the performance is taking place.

Such broadcasts had their genesis in performances that were displayed on large screens in public areas, often for free. The Royal Opera was an innovator in this endeavor, regularly showing telecasts of live performances on a large screen erected outside the Royal Opera House. Hundreds of people would gather in front of that screen, many with a drink from a local pub in hand. This audience would watch in rapt silence, applaud at the appropriate times, and cheer loudly when, after curtain calls inside the house, the singers would bow especially for them. Despite a large public subsidy, the Royal Opera House had developed an elitist image, in part because of very high ticket prices. This attempt at eradicating that image was largely successful. Many other institutions copied this practice, including the New World Symphony in Miami Beach, Florida. Its New World Center, designed by Frank Gehry, has a permanent video wall that regularly features live performances by the symphony, as well as movies and other presentations.

The Metropolitan Opera, under the leadership of Peter Gelb, took this practice one step further, broadcasting live performances not on video walls or outdoor screens but in movie theaters, with excellent sound and high-definition images. A seat for one of these performances is a bargain compared with the price of a ticket to the opera itself. (A broadcast ticket typically costs about twenty-five dollars, while a good seat at the Met can cost hundreds of dollars.)

The broadcasts are of very high quality. And since filming allows for close-ups at key moments, one certainly has a more intimate experience than when seated in a very large opera house. Now available in more than sixty countries, Met broadcasts allow people throughout the nation and the world to enjoy opera of the highest level at a modest cost.

The Metropolitan Opera also has created Met Opera on Demand, an online subscription service that allows subscribers to view performances from its archive. Other institutions also have begun to stream broadcasts on the Internet. Some institutions, like the Vienna State Opera and the Berlin Philharmonic, require paid subscriptions to their streamed performances; others, including the Chicago Symphony Orchestra and Detroit Symphony Orchestra, offer that service free of charge.

These new forms of arts distribution have been embraced by opera companies, theater companies, ballet companies, and symphonies. While television broadcasts of such performances have not proven popular enough to attract advertising dollars, the target audiences for theater and online broadcasts seem happy to pay for the experience. These broadcasts represent the single most important change in the way arts have been distributed since the mid-twentieth century.

And they have mammoth implications for the arts in general.

Local arts organizations must now compete with the world's best-known institutions for the attention of their local audience. While it is difficult to compare attending a performance in person with a performance on screen, for many people the difference in cost—and in quality—is worth moving from three dimensions to two. The Metropolitan Opera's production values are so high that—even on a screen—the sets and costumes can look more spectacular than those of a local opera company. The Met's singers have more star power than their local counterparts. Theater audio systems deliver excellent sound quality. And one needs neither a hard-to-get reservation nor an expensive ticket.

What we have learned in other settings is that changes in distribution networks can revolutionize an industry. The pantyhose industry is a good case in point. Until the 1970s, women purchased stockings in department stores at very high prices. There were literally hundreds of styles, colors, and textures. Although many manufacturers made stockings, all of the companies were relatively small. Then the Hanes Corporation decided to reduce the number of styles dramatically, package their pantyhose in a plastic egg, and distribute them through drug stores and other less expensive outlets—reducing cost by a large factor. Hundreds of small manufacturers were unable to compete and the industry was changed forever. Similar shifts have occurred over the past century in automobiles and auto parts, banking services, food services, office supplies, and building supplies. In every case, the number of competitors was reduced and customers got products and services at far lower costs.

Why does this happen? Because industries change as consumers make decisions about what they want, what price they are willing to pay, and how they wish their goods or services to be delivered.

As industries mature, their products nearly always become standardized. As a product moves from being a specialty (where different sets of consumers demand different features, raising the costs of production and increasing the price of the item) to becoming a commodity (where mass production and distribution reduce the cost per unit), prices invariably fall. And if costs fall substantially enough, customers can be willing to forgo some previously desirable features. Those of us who lived through the Japanese invasion of the automobile industry will remember that, at the time (the 1970s and 1980s), Japanese imports offered few custom features, but the cars were of good quality. And they were cheap.

This sort of standardization happens in industry after industry —a result of growing price sensitivity in buyers and the cost reductions allowed by economies of scale.

THE COMMODITIZATION OF THE ARTS

While many industries mature in this fashion as demand grows and the number of manufacturers diminishes, those of us who work in the arts have argued for decades that our industry is different. Art will never be a commodity, we declare, because every production is different. Our performers are individual artists and that means, by definition, we will continue to offer a highly differentiated product. For example, how could an educated operagoer confuse the Metropolitan Opera's production of *Der Rosenkavalier* with the Paris Opera's production of the same work? And the Chicago Symphony just doesn't sound like the Philadelphia Orchestra; anyone can tell that!

While such comments might have been accepted without disagreement in the 1950s, '60s, and '70s—when we truly had both a large, educated audience that could discern differences between performances and a host of stars in every genre—the situation is not the same today. Take opera, for instance. In the 1970s, I routinely heard the best singers in the world at the Metropolitan Opera, including Joan Sutherland, Leontyne Price, Birgit Nilsson, Montserrat Caballé, Marilyn Horne, Plácido Domingo, Luciano Pavarotti, and Sherrill Milnes. (And this was not even considered the Golden Age of singing!) Many of these performers were household names, featured on television and in recordings, and paid for promotional appearances. And, indeed, to a large portion of the audience, a performance of *Aida* with Leontyne Price was a completely different experience than *Aida* with Birgit Nilsson.

Although we also have remarkable singers today, the recording industry is not the same as it was thirty years ago. The introduction of CDs that rarely broke or were scratched (and therefore didn't need to be replaced), followed by the growth of iPods and other music players that allowed consumers to purchase and share individual tracks (once again the move to bite-size experiences rears its head), resulted in the near-death of the recording industry. Without this for-profit partner, opera companies (or symphonies) can't mount as intense an effort to make stars of the singers (or conductors or orchestral soloists) as they did in the past. And the declining profitability of popular music means the recording industry has even less room for losses on their classical music operations. Many companies have shut them down entirely.

We also do not have Ed Sullivan promoting the very best performers. Or Merv Griffin. Or Mike Douglas. Most viewers have never heard an opera singer or a classical musician on television and could not name one performing on stage today.

As a result, only a handful of today's stars can routinely sell out a performance. Of the artists I listed from the 1970s, only Plácido Domingo is still actively performing, and he does so far less frequently than before. Yo-Yo Ma, Renée Fleming, and a few other performers are very well known, but that list is small and dwindling. This places great pressure on arts organizations to build name recognition for their artists. That task can be difficult enough for resident artists; it can be even harder for guests, who typically appear for only a few performances. Why invest heavily to promote someone who may be gone the following week?

We are suffering an even more dramatic decline in the fame of ballet dancers and choreographers, not to mention modern dance artists. In the 1960s and 1970s, a number of highly visible Russian ballet dancers defected to the West, including Rudolf Nureyev, Mikhail Baryshnikov, and Natalia Makarova. Although these were extraordinary artists, they also became front-page news stories—a fact that only heightened their fame. These dancers were routinely interviewed on popular television shows and featured in big studio movies. Today, artists must establish celebrity on their own. There are many astonishingly talented ballet dancers today—David Hallberg, Natalia Osipova, and Tiler Peck among them—but they have not achieved the level of recognition that previous stars attained. While they continue to appear in ballet performances in the world's great theaters, they are rarely seen on television or other popular entertainment media.

This problem extends to ballet choreographers as well. Perhaps two choreographers—Alexei Ratmansky and Christopher Wheeldon—have achieved star status in ballet. But even their premieres do not create the excitement that their predecessors—George Balanchine, Jerome Robbins, Sir Frederick Ashton, and Anthony Tudor—expected.

In modern dance, the situation is yet more dire. Of the giants who created a thriving field—Martha Graham, Merce Cunningham, Alvin Ailey, Paul Taylor, Twyla Tharp, and others—only a few are still working, and none could be said to be in their prime. There are many wonderful younger choreographers, of course, but none of them has established a company of the stature of these greats except for Mark Morris (who, it must be said, is nearing his sixtieth birthday). The future of modern dance is uncertain. There is no doubt that the field will survive with a large number of smaller organizations. But without at least a few major companies, it is doubtful that enough money will be contributed to keep the field as large, as visible, and as potent as it became in the twentieth century.

The dance world also faces one more threat. Until twenty years ago, most dancers would work with one company for their entire careers. Although a dancer might occasionally guest star with another company, it was considered important to learn one particular style and to work with a single artistic leader. There were notable exceptions, of course—the defecting Russians obviously had to change companies (and Baryshnikov changed companies several times)—but the vast majority of dancers remained loyal to one company. Increasingly, we now see dancers, particularly star dancers, spreading their allegiance among several dance organizations. David Hallberg is a principal dancer with both American Ballet Theatre and the Bolshoi Ballet (the only foreign-born principal dancer in the history of the Bolshoi); he also guest stars with other companies. Natalia Osipova danced for both American Ballet Theatre and the Bolshoi, then moved to the Mikhailovsky Ballet, and is now a member of the Royal Ballet in London.

And it is not only principal dancers who are willing to travel. The corps de ballet of many companies boasts dancers from a United Nations of ballet schools. As a result, the differences among ballet companies are beginning to wane. The distinctions among Russian, English, Italian, and French styles (satirized in Tudor's *Gala Performance*) are beginning to disappear. Not only are major ballet companies starting to look alike, they also are dancing the same repertory. One can now see Balanchine's major dances performed across the globe. (I have seen *Jewels* alone performed by seven different companies.)

This sort of globalization also exists in the other arts, of course.

For the past century, many opera singers have performed in houses around the world, while today's opera producers also work in many countries. One can hear Valery Gergiev conduct on three continents in one week and—if the right technology is available—see productions by Francesca Zambello in Moscow, London, Washington, and Cooperstown on the same date!

For all of these reasons, differentiation in the arts is evaporating. Increasingly, we can discern a sameness to the arts across companies and even countries.

THE KINKED DEMAND CURVE

Business theory teaches us that when products begin to look alike, the price sensitivity of buyers increases, economies of scale play a larger role, and there are clear winners and losers. And while most industries follow that trend, most also retain a specialty segment that caters to customers who are willing to pay more for additional features.

So while the airline industry sells the vast majority of its seats to cost-conscious purchasers—spawning the creation of Southwest Airlines, JetBlue, and other discount airlines—a smaller group of customers is willing to pay for business or first-class seats and an even smaller segment prefers to buy its own airplanes.

We did not experience this development in the arts. We saw the creation of thousands of arts organizations, often presenting similar products. But because the distribution of those products was so localized, we were more like the old-fashioned market for ladies' stockings than the new, standardized panty hose industry. Local organizations made products for local consumption, with some touring activity but not enough to dent the sales of other organizations. For many years, in fact, touring was on the wane, as the cost of moving a large ensemble had grown too high. The cancellation of the Metropolitan Opera tour in 1986, for example, signaled a reduction in the competition from national powerhouses and the rise of regionalization. No longer would the entire company set up shop in Boston, New Orleans, or Denver for a week or two, with the associated opportunities for galas, parties, and the like. When the Met tour was cancelled, local opera patrons had little choice but to support their home companies.

But now we have the Met's movie-theater broadcasts and, on the horizon, a rapid increase in Internet broadcasts. (Union artists will be pressured to participate in this new mode of distribution at a modest increase in salaries.) Internet broadcasts could take the impact of movie-theater presentations one step further. People could watch in their homes (or offices, or cars, or trains) at a time that was convenient for them. Just as Netflix has changed television and movie-viewing habits, Internet broadcasts of arts events could give consumers the chance to watch on their own time, at their own pace. It is entirely possible that movie-theater broadcasts will be a transitional product. Just as the VCR was a step between traditional television viewing and DVR technology—and Netflix now streams movies rather than mailing DVDs—movie-theater broadcasts may be a only first step toward distributing the arts online and on demand.

It has yet to be determined how these new distribution methods will affect the future of the arts in this nation and abroad. Will they cannibalize the audience for local performances? Do they represent a new version of the Metropolitan Opera on tour, sapping attention and money from regional institutions? Or will they educate and entice a new generation of opera lovers? Will the demand for local opera increase after people are introduced to opera through these excellent, inexpensive broadcasts? Will the broadcasting technology only be affordable for a few, select institutions? Will this spell the end of mid-sized arts organizations, those with a relatively large infrastructure but the inability to take advantage of new technologies? Such speculation is left for the next chapter. Whatever the impact, it will be momentous and industry-altering. Anyone who suggests otherwise should study the development of other industries. The arts are special but they are not immune from change.

One aspect of the arts that is truly different from other industries is the range of its customers' price sensitivity. While virtually every buyer would rather pay less than more for a given seat at the theater, the degree to which price determines whether a seat will

KINKED DEMAND CURVE

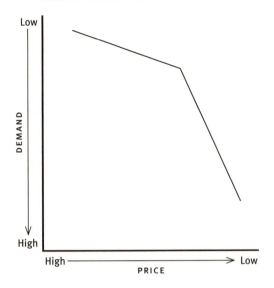

be purchased varies wildly. Although most of our patrons care very much about ticket prices, there are segments of our audience that do not worry about them at all. One board member at American Ballet Theatre told me that the way to balance our budget was to double our ticket prices since he did not care how much he spent on them. (The same board member routinely bought two tickets on the Concorde for himself, so that he would not be crowded by the hoi polloi.)

The arts typically have a kinked demand curve—meaning that the price sensitivity of the higher-end customers is substantially lower than that of those who buy cheaper seats. This is the reason that Broadway shows can sell premium seats—often costing many hundreds of dollars—while most seats cost only a fraction of that price. (The same reasoning applies to sports fans and luxury skyboxes.)

This situation creates a wide chasm between audience types, a chasm that is mirrored in all aspects of our society. While most arts organizations have a mission to serve all audiences, the pressure to attract those with great resources can often get in the way of efforts to attract those of more modest means. Since more arts organizations are struggling to survive — and therefore urgently desire to raise more funds — the impetus to create and market events that appeal to the well-to-do is increasing. Of course, it is the larger, more illustrious organizations that have an easier time attracting this segment.

The ability of the biggest and best-financed arts institutions to produce grand and exciting works, to mount major marketing campaigns, to broadcast their works to large audiences, and to access the wealthiest patrons, gives them advantages that increasingly separates them from smaller, less well-resourced organizations.

NEW MODELS

As the gulf between the haves and the have-nots widens — and a few giant organizations emerge as "winners" — a number of smaller, more nimble ventures also should develop. These ventures will be far more flexible than the behemoth organizations, and will typically serve a very particular customer set.

In the automobile industry, the giants such as General Motors, Toyota, and Ford serve the mass market. But there also are very specialized car manufacturers — like Lamborghini and Maserati — which serve the very demanding and rich, and others — like Kia and Mitsubishi — which serve the ultra price-conscious.

In the arts, we have already seen pop-up operas, individual theater projects (often in site-specific locations), pick-up modern dance ensembles, and random acts of culture. It would not be possible to do grand opera, classical ballet, or classical symphony orchestra performances in this manner, of course, as these require a large group that rehearses and performs together frequently to establish a high level of quality. But many creative artists are making work that can be performed in non-traditional locations by smaller ensembles; this is an artistic choice that is often driven by economic necessity.

The wish to develop these mini-projects has coincided with the desire of many younger artists to be independent of large institutions, to have the freedom to move from project to project with relative abandon. This movement has facilitated many interdisciplinary projects that have been both innovative and exciting. But there is a cost. Every time such a project is developed, the creators must start anew to build an audience and a donor base. One advantage of an ongoing arts institution is that it can create a family of supporters who stay with the organization as it moves from project to project. The allegiance of the audience and the donors is not to a given project, but to the organization itself. That is why the Chicago Symphony, the Royal Shakespeare Company, and other major arts institutions can continue to operate, decade after decade, even as artists and administrators are replaced. Arts organizations build families of supporters who are attracted to the work of the institution; these supporters become audience members, volunteers, donors, and even board members. These families provide both financial and moral support, serving as ambassadors for the organization in their communities. They provide a sort of insurance against disaster, whether that comes in the form of a bad season or a financial problem. And they tend to be the ones who support new ventures — new buildings, endowment drives, and major new productions. For large organizations, the donor base alone can be huge. The Kennedy Center, for example, has 30,000 donors who annually support the work of the institution! Without them, the Kennedy Center could not survive. (This population of donors will be threatened if the federal government reduces or eliminates the tax credit for charitable donations. While many donors are not motivated to give merely by the tax deductibility of their gifts, they know that the cost of making that gift has been partially offset by the tax deduction. It is simple economics to predict that, if the deduction is reduced, contributions will fall as well. At a time when arts organizations need to increase their donor bases, this could be catastrophic.)

Groups of artists who combine for one project, then disband, do not have the ability to create the same ongoing support base that long-lived institutions do. Every time they assemble a new group, they must either go back to the same set of family and friends (who will likely tire of giving over time) or seek new funders. But finding and cultivating new donors takes time and effort. And project-based programming doesn't afford much time for donor cultivation. An ongoing arts organization can (and should) be cultivating donors to support projects years into the future.

This new approach to art-making, therefore, works against traditional approaches to fund-raising. Not surprisingly, new forms of fund-raising have risen in turn. With the vital assistance of new technologies, project teams (and mainstream arts organizations too) have moved on from the long-term cultivation of donors to quicker, more anonymous forms of fund-raising, primarily through online crowdfunding mechanisms such as Kickstarter.

These online campaigns are nearly always project-focused and typically set a rather modest target for funding. Often marketed using social-media platforms—Twitter and Facebook and the like—they do not necessarily help build a family of donors, since the artists have virtually no interaction (no pun intended) with their funders.

The most productive fund-raising efforts create strong interpersonal relationships between an organization and its donors; over time, these relationships can grow and develop, resulting in larger gifts from many donors. Most mega-donors to arts institutions do not begin with a large donation; they typically make a modest initial gift, enjoy their association with the organization, make friends with board, staff, and fellow patrons, learn more about the organization over time, and build their level of giving. But this often takes years and requires repeated involvement in performances, exhibitions, special events, meetings, and discussions. It does not seem likely that a person who makes a modest contribution to a crowdfunded project will enjoy that experience in the same way or be moved to contribute a far greater amount when the artist's next project is announced.

It is especially intriguing that crowdfunding has taken hold in Europe in the past few years. Some major institutions—including the Louvre Museum in Paris—are experimenting with crowdfunding as they attempt to diversify their income in the wake of diminishing government funding. European institutions have not had to cultivate individual donors in the manner that is common in the United States. And while it is exciting that crowdfunding can provide a supplementary source of revenue, these institutions also must learn how to do more traditional forms of fund-raising if they are going to thrive. No large arts institution can survive solely on crowdfunding mechanisms; it simply takes too many $25 donors to pay the bills of a major museum, opera house, or theater company. The Louvre, for example, has an annual budget of over $350 million!

A new culture of philanthropy must be developed in Europe and other regions facing dramatic cuts in government funding. Can such a culture be created with the arms-length approach to fund-raising that characterizes crowdfunding? It seems unlikely at best. The culture of philanthropy we enjoy in the United States is largely a result of social activity. Arts organizations (and other not-for-profits) help define the social lives of their donors. Just as sports teams make their fans feel part of a larger family, arts organizations create social groups who value their association both with the organization and with other patrons. When enough institutions create these social groups, participation becomes a social norm. Crowdfunding does not seem to create a social life or social network away from the Internet. Like much of our online involvement, it focuses on the individual: what one person wants, when he or she wants it.

AUDIENCE ENGAGEMENT

At the same time that arts organizations have been turning to remote sources of funding, they also have been concerned with audience engagement. Ironically, the discussion about audience engagement suggests arts organizations must do more to build links to their audiences. For decades, institutional missions have included building participation levels, engaging audiences in art-making, and providing opportunities for education. These are the goals of most organizations. The Kennedy Center, for instance, has had a division called Performing Arts for Everyone since 1997; this program organizes daily free concerts and special festivals that engage the public. It appears that the current discussion of audience engagement is really an admission of failure: too many people feel like the arts are irrelevant to them and therefore are not getting involved.

Increasingly, the general public is questioning whether the arts are really for them — owing to lack of knowledge, high ticket prices, and the popularity of competing forms of entertainment. Some arts organizations have indeed done more to attract audiences, by staging performances outside of normal venues, conducting on-line contests, and other means. While these efforts are certainly laudable, however, most efforts to engage new audiences appear paper-thin, with little real investment in building *sustained* relationships. Too many of these activities fail to build true arts participation because they feel like gimmicks; such efforts simply sell a few more tickets in a given fiscal year or please a concerned donor.

There are exceptions, of course. ArtPrize, the visual arts festival held annually in Grand Rapids, Michigan, is a model for effective audience engagement. Each year, visual artists from around the world submit their works for display throughout the city. The public is invited to view the art and to vote for their favorites. The winners of the public vote, as well as those selected by a jury of experts, receive substantial awards. For a two-week period, thousands of citizens become arts lovers. The streets are filled with people going from venue to venue, and every restaurant is filled with diners discussing their favorite works. Journalists descend from around the globe to discuss the ArtPrize phenomenon.

I have to believe that a large portion of the population of Grand Rapids has learned more about the arts from ArtPrize than they have from any other vehicle. Because of their ArtPrize experiences, they have developed a sustained interest in visual arts and are far more likely to visit another museum exhibition. It is this kind of innovative project that builds arts audiences.

THE DECLINE IN ARTS EDUCATION

One approach that does not build audiences is the moral argument that "the arts are good for the community" and therefore deserve support. Such arguments — heard in public-service announcements, political lobbying efforts, and countless community meetings — only resonate with those who already believe them. This is especially true of efforts to support arts education in the public schools.

Unfortunately, we have seen a steady decline in the quality and amount of arts education in most communities. Rather than make the arts a part of the standard curriculum, most school systems leave arts education up to the individual teacher. If a third-grade teacher enjoys and appreciates the arts, for example, the students might visit a museum, put on a class play, or host a visiting artist. These same children might then have a fourth-grade teacher who does not understand the arts; in that case, they will have virtually no arts participation for the year.

We do not teach any other subject in this inconsistent manner. We expect our children to receive a systematic, sustained education in mathematics, science, reading, and English, regardless of the interests of the individual teacher. But we allow this helter-skelter approach to arts education. As a result, we are not truly educating our children to think of the arts as a vital, consistent part of their lives, nor are students benefiting from the sustained opportunity to exercise their creativity — an essential part of success in today's economy. We no longer live in a manufacturing environment. We must train students to participate fully and actively in a creative economy; involvement in the arts is an inexpensive and effective way to do this.

While many arts organizations have worked hard to develop programming that can fill the gap left by diminishing formal education in the schools, the students who participate in this programming do not often experience it as part of a comprehensive arts curriculum; instead, they merely enjoy a day at the theater or a trip to a museum.

As arts education continues to be de-emphasized, the educational establishment — spurred by politicians and the business community — has placed increasing emphasis on the so-called STEM fields (science, technology, engineering, and mathematics). In their view, the future of the economy rests on these four areas. A balanced education—including literature, history, and the arts—is now considered a luxury. Though many successful scientists, engineers, and mathematicians think that STEM should be STEAM—with the addition of the arts—they are in the minority.

THE DECLINE IN ARTS JOURNALISM

At the same time that arts education has been in decline (or perhaps because of this decline), we also are witnessing a dramatic reduction in the amount of serious arts criticism in our nation's newspapers.

Many people no longer get their news from a daily paper; they read news online, throughout the day, whenever it is convenient for them, on one of literally thousands of Web sites that provide information on current events. Not surprisingly, the traditional newspaper industry has suffered tremendously. For the same reasons that arts organizations are doing less advertising in their local newspapers, other industries are as well. It is expensive compared with online advertising and, as the reader base diminishes, hardcopy advertising pays off less and less. This has hurt the profitability of the newspaper and magazine industry.

As a result, newspapers everywhere are looking for ways to reduce costs. Numerous journalists are losing their jobs, news bureaus are being closed, and the quality of journalism is suffering. As participation in the classical arts has waned, eliminating serious arts coverage has become a favored technique for saving money. In recent years, numerous periodicals have reduced arts coverage, often substantially. Even the *New York Times* now devotes an increasing percentage of its "arts" coverage to popular music, movies, and television. In most publications, popular culture so dominates the discussion that coverage of ballet, opera, theater, dance, and the visual arts are relegated to the back pages. Although many of the journalists no longer employed by newspapers and magazines now have online blogs and columns, their readership and impact have been vastly reduced. This also has reduced the visibility of the arts themselves, creating a truly vicious cycle.

This decrease in professional criticism in print has occurred as online networks make it far easier for amateur critics to build a platform. While this development encourages more audience engagement and showcases the opinions of many knowledgeable individuals, it also allows for anonymous, ill-informed criticism and reduces the impact of the professional critics who possess the knowledge and standards that could educate audiences and pressure artists to deliver their best work. On first reading, it is often difficult to know which critics have the depth of knowledge and insight to be believed. And the sheer number of online critiques is so large that they can become a blur, perhaps creating an impression but not really educating as the best critics do.

THE GATHERING STORM

It is not surprising that, as arts offerings become more commodified, risk-taking is avoided, the press is less involved, and alternate forms of entertainment are more prevalent, many arts organizations are facing substantial deficits. These organizations frequently blame "the economy," but the truth is far more complex. In just the past few years, we have lost Opera Pacific, the Baltimore Opera, Opera Boston, Opera San Antonio, and the New York City Opera. Although the economy played a role in the demise of each of these institutions, it was clearly not the only factor in any of them.

It must be restated here that not every arts organization has succumbed to the pressures I've described. There are many well-managed, exciting, and well-marketed organizations that have created large families of supporters. These organizations have been weathering the storm quite well, thank you.

But they are in the minority. A larger group of arts organizations is hanging on, limping from one season to the next, depleting reserves and lines of credit, losing the support of their tired family members, and relying on heroic giving by a few loyal donors. The ones in the worst shape are cutting back on programming, raiding their endowments, eliminating cash reserve funds, or simply not paying their bills.

As the financial challenges to arts organizations continue to mount, as demand shrinks in a world without arts education, and as competing forms of entertainment emerge—produced by highly efficient and well-capitalized corporations—an increasing number of loyalists and sponsors are beginning to question the basic model of arts organizations. That this is happening during a period of fiscal instability is not a coincidence. Wealthy individuals have been growing uncertain about their own sources of income; the pressure to economize comes from many different sides. Increasingly, corporations are improving the bottom line by becoming far more productive. Corporate wealth is growing but wages are not, with more work placed in the hands of less expensive offshore or part-time employees.

All of this creates an environment in which board members and donors (who are often the beneficiaries of corporate success if not corporate leaders themselves) are evaluating the challenges of the arts organizations they support far more carefully. The phrase "All arts organizations have deficits" is no longer acceptable to many boards, who are quickly becoming divided between deficit hawks and arts enthusiasts.

The arts enthusiasts are quick to defend the artistic prerogatives of the organization's leadership; they argue that cutting anything related to art will only weaken the organization. This group believes they are the protectors of the organization's mission. They don't really care about balance sheets and believe fervently that artistic accomplishment is worth any financial challenge. They remain convinced that the organization will get by despite cash shortfalls.

The deficit hawks, on the other hand, believe that the only way to truly protect the organization's mission is to ensure that organization itself survives. They believe that creating a sustainable organization requires changing its business model—a fancy way of saying "cutting costs to the bone." But this is not a viable long-term strategy. One can only cut so many programs before the organization barely seems to exist (like the New York City Opera). For many arts organizations, especially those that maintain large ensembles—of performers, stagehands, technical staff, and so on—the only way to cut budgets substantially (after programming is decimated) is to reduce salaries.

In many arts organizations, the deficit hawks have forced furloughs or wage and hiring freezes. These measures typically reduce morale substantially, without saving the large amounts that are often needed. In other organizations, even more drastic measures have been sought, including huge cuts in salaries. Not surprisingly, symphony orchestras have witnessed the most hawkish behavior. As previously noted, orchestras suffer from the productivity issue more than other arts organizations. They are the least flexible and the least visually oriented, and are losing their audiences more quickly. Because musician salaries comprise a huge portion of the budget, it is no wonder that board members who are looking to make substantial cuts focus attention there. And it does not help that executive leadership is typically frustrated (to say the least), with the restrictive covenants of a collective bargaining agreement.

We have seen major cuts demanded in Detroit, Indianapolis, and elsewhere. But the Minnesota Orchestra has become the poster child for the ambitions of the deficit hawks. Led by two bankers, the board locked out the musicians after demanding that they take draconian cuts in salary. The musicians argued, rather effectively, that the problem lay not with their salaries but with poor executive management. Unable to build a sufficient family of donors, the orchestra instead overdrew from its endowment to cover operating losses. Adding insult to injury was a "successful" $50 million campaign to renovate Orchestra Hall. If things were so bad, argued the musicians, why was this money used to tart up a venue instead of securing the organization's health?

Good question.

The public, somewhat surprisingly, sided with the musicians. So many American workers have taken wage cuts as a result of the loss of manufacturing jobs that they often cannot feel sympathy for musicians who earn well over $100,000 a year. But this was not the case in Minnesota. Whether this was because of the acclaim enjoyed by the orchestra, the spectacle of a few highly compensated business executives trying to reduce the wages of others, or a mishandled public-relations effort, the board of the Minnesota Orchestra came under fire. In the end, they settled for a much smaller reduction in wages than originally proposed.

This "victory" by the musicians may be pyrrhic. They may maintain most of their salaries but lose a group of donors and board members—the group who were convinced that anything short of major reductions would spell the end of the orchestra. The huge crowds that have flocked to the musicians' ad hoc concerts may lose interest, and their contributions may not cover the loss of the departed donors.

Only time will tell.

....

Curtains?

BRAVE NEW WORLD,

PART I

THE ARTS IN AMERICA IN 2035

Over the coming two decades, the trends that began (or have been accelerating) since the year 2000 will create a new arts ecology in this country and abroad. Improvements in technology coupled with new distribution methods will alter both arts institutions and arts programming. A second generation of children without substantial arts education in the schools will reduce demand for the classical arts. And the aging of our donor base and audience will create financial instability throughout the sector.

Of course, people will always have a need to express themselves —regardless of race, economic status, or educational level. The cave dwellers of Lascaux demonstrated this over 17,000 years ago. The drawings there are monuments to a human desire to comment on our surroundings. We can see in our mind's eye the great painting, sculpture, architecture, dance, music, and theater that have emerged from every era in history—from the ancient Greeks to the Renaissance Italians to the Tudor English. There is no scenario which suggests that arts-making will stop.

People in the future may have different tastes, but they will still need to express their opinions on life, love, and their environment in song, movement, picture, and word. Live performances will still happen, but there might be fewer of the large ensemble casts that we enjoy now. The cost of mounting such performances, the ready availability of cheaper substitutes, and the accessibility of excellent online performances will work to reduce the number of live-and-in-person events. And such events will be expensive—tickets will cost up to $1000 each for performances by major groups, limiting demand to the very wealthy or the truly passionate, with even the biggest devotees able to attend only a few events per year.

With fewer performances, arts institutions will become less reliant on ticket sales and more dependent on fund-raising. This trend has already been in evidence. Twenty years ago, the Metropolitan Opera earned 60 percent of its total revenue from ticket sales. In 2012, that figure was only 27.6 percent, with 44 percent coming from fund-raising and 10 percent from its movie-theater broadcasts. And while the Metropolitan Opera may be one of the largest performing arts institutions, it is certainly not the only one to experience this decline in ticket sales.

Long before 2035, it is likely that many more productions will be available for viewing at home, on demand. While these performances should attract sizeable audiences, there will be a reduction in overall demand for the classical arts, owing to another two decades without comprehensive arts education and the passing away of many current arts lovers and supporters. Far fewer donors will want to support the arts. The people who will be forty-five to sixty-five years old in 2035 are now in their late twenties and early thirties. As they represent the first modern American generation that did not receive systematic arts education, they are likely to dedicate their philanthropy to other sectors, including healthcare, education, and social services. Most of the support for the arts that remains will go to the largest institutions, which will have national and international impact through their broadcasts. These groups will benefit from high visibility, potent fund-raising mechanisms, and strong boards. Such assets will make them attractive to funders motivated by the desire for social status and access to famous artists.

This does not mean that diverse sectors of the population will not remain involved in the arts. People will continue to sing and dance and paint and act. There will be smaller professional and community-based organizations that cater to local audiences; these will provide outlets for new artists and new art forms. Such organizations will always exist, giving citizens and local performers the opportunity to flex their creative muscles.

There also will be a host of computer-driven tools that allow people to write, compose, act, sing, and perform music. Although the antecedents of these tools already exist, they will be improved substantially. People will conduct virtual orchestras, act in movies (replete with special effects), design theater sets and costumes, and compose opera scores in their living rooms. They will be able to record the results and share them with friends via new online social networking platforms. The millennial generation has demonstrated a great love of participation. They have been distinguished by their community spirit and performed a great deal of volunteer work, even as young teens. They also enjoy and expect active participation in their entertainment—they vote for their favorite singers online, play interactive games, and enjoy performances that feature audience participation. The availability of these astonishing methods for making art will present cheap, convenient, and engaging substitutes to buying tickets to performances.

Some of these home-generated performances will "go viral," becoming even more popular than the performances broadcast by large institutions. In 2011, the Metropolitan Opera broadcasts reached 3 million viewers; the following year over 1 *billion* people watched a YouTube video featuring the South Korean singer Psy! When the average person can create a video with special effects, high production values, and full musical accompaniment, the number of competitive online offerings will become huge.

Many other forms of entertainment will be available online. There will be numerous "stories" not created originally for television or the movies, such as the Netflix series *House of Cards*, which has won several Emmy awards. These also will be special productions, not unlike the live broadcast of *The Sound of Music* with Carrie Underwood; these will be created for online sales, however, without the backing of a television network. To consumers, such backing will be irrelevant. Writers and directors will be especially prized. Such stories may actually appear to "happen" in your home—through the use of holographic technology. One might get to see the murdered corpse in your living room, then have the chance to solve the crime by interviewing suspects as they sit before you, and examining the evidence yourself. It will be difficult for a small modern dance group to compete with that!

New books and music will be available on demand, as will concerts and other performances. Higher-definition screens with higher-quality sound duplication will make concerts and other musical events far more satisfying. Speaker design and configuration will make it feel like one is truly there in the live audience, replicating the overtones that we feel inside the concert hall. Although traditional movies will still be available, they will be streamed, on demand, to our computers and mobile devices. It is not a certainty that movie theaters will continue to exist, however, let alone movie-theater broadcasts of opera, theater, or ballet. Virtually every device will be voice-actuated, if not thought-activated; the argument over which kind of keypad works best will likely be moot.

Home theaters will be the norm, with customized seating, screens, and sound systems all controlled by a single, simple device. Headphones will not be necessary to avoid offending the neighbors, as the directional speakers will only be heard by those in a specific location.

As communications and teleconferencing systems improve, telecommuting will become far more common. With more people working from their homes, this will lower the costs of commuting and reduce the need for business travel. And with home theaters and vastly expanded home shopping capabilities, people will have few other incentives to venture out.

With all of these new tools, arts participation will become as solitary as enjoying one's iPad is today. Technology will make communications far easier, reducing the need for social interactions in public places. Some people may still enjoy congregating to share an entertainment experience, but current trends do not suggest that they will represent the majority of Americans. The cost of maintaining a theater will have to be spread over a smaller base of ticket buyers, meaning ticket costs will go up and watching a performance in public will be considered a luxury.

Along with sporting events and religion, the arts had been one of the few activities that people did together. But technology has given us the ability to do whatever we chose, at our own time and pace. Even in 2013, sports "participation" increasingly meant watching at home. Ticket prices were so high, travel felt like a waste, and HD television changed the home viewing experience. At-home viewing allowed for additional features not available at the game itself. The RedZone package, for example, showed any NFL football game in which a team was within the twenty-yard line of its opponent (and thus facing a scoring opportunity). One no longer had to watch an entire football game in order to enjoy the highlights.

Following a similar model, opera buffs will tune in the highlights instead of waiting for *Celeste Aida* or *La donna è mobile*. Even church services will be "delivered" for home viewing, as organized religions will forfeit the sanctity of a house of worship in order to attract more followers.

Although museums will remain the secure repositories of great artistic and historical objects, it will no longer be necessary to visit a museum to see a curated exhibition. These will be distributed on demand to our computers, along with large quantities of supporting materials—letters, historical documents, maps, and other types of information. One will even be able to curate one's own exhibition by assembling the works one wishes to display and providing commentary; such exhibitions will be shared online as well. Advances in holographic technology will enable sculptures to be "displayed" in one's living room in three dimensions. Because it also will be possible to beam the great performers of the past and present into our living rooms, the now unlikely scenario of Michael Jackson dancing next to the Winged Victory could become a commonplace reality.

One of the reasons that people will not attend as many public performances is because they will be working harder; spending more hours at their computers and having even less predictable time off. In 2013, new communications and Internet technologies already meant that everyone was available all of the time. People were texting on ski slopes and at the gym. One could attend a theater performance and, at intermission, watch a sizable portion of the audience use their smartphones until the curtain rose again. In many instances, they were transacting some form of business. But people in 2035 will not be earning more in order to live a life of leisure, they will be earning more simply to earn more.

This will result, in part, from changing goals and ambitions. In the 1950s, the American dream consisted of a comfortable middle-class home with two cars in the garage. In the latter half of the twentieth century, that dream changed to becoming a millionaire. By 2010, people dreamed of being billionaires, and there were already many in our midst (the U.S. total was 442). Achieving this level of wealth requires a focus and dedication not often in evidence fifty years earlier.

By 2035, there will likely be little or no formal arts education available in our public schools. While both educators and industry leaders will recognize the value of arts education to developing a creative workforce, school systems simply will not have adequate budgets. The funds required to pay the health-care and living expenses of the aged will be astronomical. With no political will to deal with these costs, government funding for anything other than absolute necessities will be cut to the bone. Online arts education will have to suffice, augmented by the efforts of arts institutions to fill the breach. But without organized effort, these episodic encounters will not create the arts background that will nurture a significant involvement with the arts. Where will the audiences, volunteers, donors, and board members of the future come from? Will the donor base become too narrow just at the time when arts organizations will be most dependent on fund-raising? Will this mean that only a few arts organizations can truly prosper?

There will, of course, be many people who still love the arts. Unfortunately, there will simply be a lot fewer of them as a percentage of the total population. These will be the lucky ones who were exposed to the arts as children; the ones whose parents and teachers loved the arts and wanted to ensure that their children had the same opportunities as they did.

Demographic trends will affect whether parents have the time and money to bring the arts to their children. There is already a growing bifurcation in the ages of U.S. parents. Many are having children when they are very young, while another segment is waiting longer to form their families. Over one-third of U.S. residents in 2010 had at least one child before the age of twenty (and 79 percent of these were unmarried). For a high percentage of these teenage parents, the arts will be unaffordable. Young parents must work hard just to take care of basic needs and do not often get the education they need to create a more secure lifestyle for themselves and their children. Even with a desire to introduce their children to the arts, the disposable time will simply not be available.

For those who wait until their thirties and beyond to have children, finances may be less of an issue. But will there be the necessary love for the arts? Will there be time to bring the children to piano lessons and ballet class? Or will their careers be so demanding — and interest in the arts so low — that their children will be offered other, more easily delivered forms of entertainment? Will parents whose interests lie elsewhere feel the pressure to introduce their children to flute lessons and acting classes? It seems unlikely.

PERFORMANCES IN 2035

Besides reducing the demand for seats at performances, these trends also will decrease interest in classes, workshops, and other sources of auxiliary income, which will cause additional fiscal problems for arts organizations. As these organizations face financial challenges, they will be motivated to offer less programming overall, as well as less challenging or surprising work. This will make the arts look dull compared to other entertainment options and will weaken demand even more. This vicious spiral will result in the demise of many arts organizations.

Those performances that still occur are likely to fall into one of two basic categories. The most visible will be those featuring world-class and world-famous organizations and stars. While a lucky few might be able to afford tickets to see these performances in person, most people will be watching them in their own homes. These events will be mounted only in large venues, in important cities, and will be extremely expensive. In 2013, Broadway theaters already could charge up to $600 for a ticket to a show featuring a celebrated actor, and the Metropolitan Opera charged $300 for an orchestra seat on a regular basis. Even regional companies such as the Seattle Opera, Minnesota Opera, and Florida Grand Opera had seats that sold for over $200 a performance. One can only imagine how expensive tickets will be in the future, when there are fewer performances available and we have experienced another two decades of inflation.

The second kind of performance will consist of relatively low-budget productions with modest ticket prices, for which artists will be paid poorly if at all. These will feature local artists with an earnest desire to express themselves and groups of young performers for whom this is the only way to gain experience. Many of the organizations that produce such programming will be short-lived. With modest management resources, an absence of stars, and a limited amount of publicity, it will be difficult for them to establish a substantial donor base. This will make it simply too hard to maintain operations. These smaller groups will work extremely hard to mount a performance; they will struggle to build an audience, earn only a pittance, and fail to attract a base large enough to make the next production better and more profitable. Many will last for a season or two, then quietly disband in pursuit of more sustainable ventures. For many people living outside of major cities — and those in major cities without access to a great deal of disposable income — these groups are likely to provide the only opportunities to see live performances on a regular basis.

It will be difficult for arts organizations that are now considered "mid-sized" to prosper. Local performances will satisfy the needs of many in the audience, and online performances by the largest institutions will dominate the media, viewed by hundreds of thousands — if not millions — of people. Creating an audience base of people willing to leave their homes for a mid-level performance will be difficult. More challenging still will be the task of finding enough donors who know about the organization, value its work, and are willing to underwrite the costs of production. While mid-sized organizations play a huge role in the current arts ecology, by 2035 they are likely to be relatively scarce.

MARKETING IN 2035

Creating visibility for arts organizations of any size will become more challenging. It isn't clear that the word "newspaper" will mean much anymore. People will receive their news online, in real time, with real-time video and commentary. There will be so many opportunities to personalize the stream of news and entertainment that it will not be attractive to read the same newspaper that someone else reads. People will get reports on those stories and topics of most interest to them, without having to sort through stories and advertisements that are of little interest.

Online news distribution also will offer greater opportunities for celebrity journalists who can forego the support of an established publication. We have already witnessed the beginning of this trend with the defections of Nate Silver from *The New York Times* to ESPN, Ezra Klein from *The Washington Post* to Vox Media, and Kara Swisher and Walt Mossberg from *The Wall Street Journal* to NBC Universal. Many journalists will come to believe they could gain a larger readership, more control over their own work, and earn far more money by becoming independent. This will create a small group of very powerful opinion-makers in all forms of journalism, including arts criticism. The resulting lack of diversity of opinion will provide a challenge for those institutions and artists not favored by the powerful few. The quantity of widely read, professional criticism will be vastly reduced, making it far harder to build visibility than it is today, especially in smaller cities.

These few, potent voices will be counterbalanced by the myriad of amateur opinions that find a presence on the Internet. It is likely that new platforms will aggregate criticism by genre and by performance; these services will provide more exposure for those writing reviews. Rating systems based on audience surveys will automatically tabulate and display information for each performance. One will not have to wait for these ratings, since they will be displayed in real time. Although there will be no shortage of opinions, there will likely be a shortage of educated and professional critics, since only those with a strong following will be able to earn a living from their reviews.

65

Brave New World, Part I

A range of devices will provide these ratings and reviews — tablets and smartphones, for the old-fashioned types, but also smart watches, online glasses, and perhaps a device that communicates through one's ear or even directly to one's brain. (This might seem improbable now but who would have predicted twenty-five years ago that a handheld device could provide access to so much online data!) The pressure to communicate immediately and to have huge quantities of data accessible at all times will only reinforce the bias for bite-sized shreds of information at the expense of in-depth analysis or reporting.

While news will be transmitted faster and more directly than ever, it is unclear what this means for the feature stories that are now so important for creating visibility in the arts. Will there still be magazines? Will short-form reporting — or tweet-like messages — replace serious arts journalism? Will feature writers find a way to be compensated for their work? Will there be enough interest in the arts to enable cadres of journalists and critics to cover local events? Or will significant arts events become so concentrated in large cities that only a small core of professional arts journalists will exist (and only in those cities)? If so, small and mid-sized organizations, as well as those in more rural areas, will find it extremely difficult to attract coverage — making it more of a challenge for any of them to gain a larger following. The press has been an important ally to many arts institutions. The visibility provided to arts events and personalities by media coverage is crucial for creating an institutional brand. If this attention is no longer available, arts institutions will lose another major support structure. (We've already lost the help of the for-profit recording industry, which has withered if not actually died.)

This will mean that arts organizations will have to create visibility entirely on their own — posing a new set of challenges for arts marketers. Creating a higher profile without the assistance of the media will force arts managers to look to other techniques. But which ones will work the best?

Direct mail will not be competitive in a world where other forms of communication are virtually free. And with the quantity of mail falling substantially, there will be fewer deliveries. (Saturday deliveries are already threatened.) Given the growing expectation that information will be available immediately, fewer delivery days reduce direct mail's potency and attractiveness even further.

Posters have never been particularly effective for selling tickets — except in very small, focused areas, such as university campuses. Reduced interest in the arts means that ticket purchasers will be even less concentrated. Marketing efforts therefore must be spread over a wider territory.

Newspaper advertising will disappear along with newspapers; if a few printed newspapers remain, their circulation will be too low to provide a significant marketing boost.

Online advertising, via e-mail blasts, Web sites, and social media platforms, will become the dominant focus of arts marketing. The total volume of online advertising will be so substantial, however, that competition for attention will be fierce. Arts institutions will have to find ways to keep their messages from being blocked by spam filters. Because social media can have an important impact on sales, campaigns to build followers will rival those to build membership levels over the past decades. Finding the optimal Web sites on which to advertise will require a great deal of data and strategy. In 2013, one could rely on the Web site of the daily newspaper to have the attention of much of the potential audience. But by 2035, no single site is likely to claim the majority of the local community; our attention will be split between hundreds of platforms and selecting the appropriate place to advertise online will be far more difficult.

Because it represents the only technique that is likely to remain potent, the amount of online arts marketing will continue to increase substantially even as the number of arts organizations falls. In this glut of messaging, smaller organizations will have a challenging time attracting any attention whatsoever. The largest institutions will be motivated to mount huge marketing efforts, not unlike the movie campaigns of today. Millions of dollars worth of sales and donations (and advertising revenue) will be at stake with every broadcast. The use of micro sites to sell productions is likely to become common. (Museums have already begun to experiment with micro sites for specific exhibitions.) Smaller organizations simply will not be able to match these campaigns. Facebook and Twitter may be extinct by 2035—we are already hearing predictions of Facebook's demise among younger users, who already prefer texting to e-mail. Over time, other platforms will emerge—each faster, more powerful, and more user-friendly than the next. Successful arts institutions will need the flexibility and capital required to move from platform to platform, taking advantage of the opportunities to reach millions of people at very low marginal cost.

ARTS EDUCATION IN 2035

Although reading and writing will remain required skills, they will recede in importance as video, audio, and holograms become the norm. Many people will still read books—literature will not become extinct—but the vast majority of books will be read online and printed books will be a luxury; bookstores will all but disappear in most cities.

The current trends in educational methodology will continue; there will be far more online learning than classroom learning, especially at the college level. With students already struggling to pay off student loans, online courses will offer a far less expensive option for earning a degree. As other efforts are made to reduce the costs of education, achieving economies of scale will be prized—lessons or lectures that can be distributed to thousands at a time via the Internet will be considered desirable.

While online learning was considered a novelty a decade ago, in twenty years it will be the norm, especially for so-called "special" subjects such as the arts; this trend will apply even at the primary-school level. Just as we expect a small group of online journalists to become stars, so will a select corps of celebrated educators. Not every university will survive; as online education becomes the norm, a few select institutions will dominate the Internet.

ORCHESTRAS IN THE FUTURE

It is highly likely that we will have fewer professional symphony orchestras in the decades to come. While community and university orchestras will continue to provide opportunities for amateur players to perform and for smaller cities to enjoy live music, one must expect that the number of professional ensembles will fall. This will, of course, reduce the number of people who have access to live performances of virtuoso musicians and further limit interest in classical music. Those who still care about the art form will be able to watch broadcasts from the several world-class ensembles that survive the shakeout, such as the Vienna Philharmonic, London Symphony Orchestra, and Los Angeles Philharmonic. This reduction in demand won't be a new phenomenon — every orchestra faces the challenge of attracting interest from an audience that increasingly turns elsewhere for entertainment. It is instructive (and depressing) to note that during one week in January 2014, the number-one selling classical album, which featured the violinist Hilary Hahn, sold only 341 copies! If this represents the baseline of interest in classical music, the future is not bright: the vast majority of classical music enthusiasts are already over the age of fifty.

In fact, it is safe to say that more than a few orchestras will go bankrupt. With demand falling and the most loyal donors passing away, several ensembles will accrue such large deficits that they simply cannot survive. This is especially likely in organizations whose boards and administrative staffs do not plan effectively for the coming changes in the arts environment. There are many who believe that programming more Beethoven and Tchaikovsky will create enough demand to enable an orchestra to survive; they are wrong.

Some boards will try the "Minnesota method" of calling for drastic salary cuts. In some cases, this will result in a serious erosion in the base of support; in others, management and musicians will fail to reach an agreement on wage reductions and the orchestra will close. The Minnesota Orchestra was such an acclaimed ensemble that politicians, journalists, and members of the public united to create pressure for a settlement on both the board and the musicians. When a similar problem is faced by a less famous orchestra, there will be fewer editorials, fewer columns, and fewer letters. It is entirely possible that the organization will simply close, without much notice. Such encounters will embolden board members of other orchestras to attempt the same approach, thinking that musicians will agree to their demands out of fear. As a result, we will witness an epidemic of labor problems in the orchestral world in the decades to come. Over time, job security likely will become the key focus of union demands in collective bargaining sessions; salary growth will be a secondary consideration.

When an orchestra closes, it is unlikely that a similar ensemble will spring up in its place. Most attempts to start new orchestras from the wreckage of old ones result in smaller, less potent groups than before. Musicians' salaries tend to fall dramatically, as the new symphonies rely a great deal on earned income at the start. Contributions to new organizations tend to be lower, and a smaller administrative staff is left to do a myriad of tasks, leaving less time for fund-raising. A healthy organization sometimes emerges over time, as was the case when the Louisiana Philharmonic Orchestra followed the demise of the New Orleans Symphony, but such resurrections will be far harder to accomplish in the future. Assembling a sufficient group of volunteers and donors will be a significant challenge in any but the largest of cities, as even a small professional orchestra will require a budget of several million dollars a year. Such ensembles—and many mid-sized orchestras as well—will find it difficult to compete effectively with broadcast concerts and other forms of entertainment. It is the largest, most prominent orchestras that will have the best chance for survival.

Some orchestras will attempt to widen their base of support by building residences in multiple cities. After the demise of the Florida Philharmonic Orchestra, for example, the Cleveland Orchestra began offering three weeks of performances in Miami each year. This move not only extends the orchestra's season, but also provides opportunities for fund-raising in the South Florida market. That only three weeks of performances satisfy demand in the region must be noted with dismay. But as more orchestras begin to close, expect the survivors to mimic this scheme.

Other orchestras will attempt to survive by merging with a near neighbor. When two orchestras perform less than 100 miles apart, for example, there will be pressure to combine operations as resources become tighter and demand remains weak. Some logical partners in the United States include Dallas and Fort Worth, and Washington, D.C., and Baltimore. It is likely that demand in one of these cities will be insufficient to support a full-time orchestra. When that occurs, a single orchestra might serve two nearby communities, giving performances, offering educational and outreach programming, and even touring on occasion. A merger would allow one set of (well paid) musicians and administrators to receive ticket revenue and donor contributions from two cities. Such arrangements would provide far more job security for musicians and allow the new institution to afford better music directors, soloists, and guest conductors. These mergers will not happen without a great deal of union and public protest, of course, but the economics suggest that this approach makes sense and, in the end, economics usually win out.

Despite modest demand, there will still be a few national and international orchestras that make recordings and videos (for electronic distribution); these activities will be viewed as essential marketing and outreach vehicles. When a high-profile orchestra, conductor, and soloist combine for an important performance, there will be demand for Internet broadcasts. Although these ventures will bring in some extra revenue for the artists, the requirement that it be "special" will be acute. In a world with an endless array of entertainment options—plus sports, politics, and news available on demand—arts programming will have to fight to stand out.

This will pressure the world-class symphonies to mount blockbuster programs in order to attract the share of online users they need to earn profits, win sponsors, and maintain visibility. We already see orchestras like the New York Philharmonic and the Los Angeles Philharmonic creating special projects out of concert productions of musicals and operas with all-star casts. Unfortunately, it is rare that a purely symphonic concert receives the same level of attention. The tension between artists (who want to perform new and adventurous repertory) and marketers, fund-raisers, and financial executives (who want to please large numbers of potential donors) will grow even more intense. When today's arts executives worry about audience, they think of a few hundred to perhaps a few thousand people. In the future, arts executives at major institutions will need to please hundreds of thousands or even millions of viewers. Their concerns for ratings will mirror those of today's major television networks.

There will be regional orchestras, to be sure, but there are likely to be far fewer of them. Musicians at most regional ensembles will only be paid for the days when they play or rehearse, receiving "per service" contracts rather than a fixed number of guaranteed weeks. As the demand for performances wanes, such guaranteed contracts will become less and less common. But moving to per service contracts will have its side effects. When musicians are paid in this way, it becomes less attractive for management to organize extensive education and outreach programs — since they must pay the musicians for each event. Those orchestras with guaranteed weeks of work can often find extra time here and there to engage musicians in outreach programs, children's performances, and so on. The reduction in outreach activities will further reduce the appreciation of classical music among young people and the underserved, causing demand to fall even further. This will affect engagement in classical music for generations to come.

For musicians, the loss of guaranteed weeks means that most will be left without a suitable income; this will force them to find auxiliary jobs, perhaps teaching music or playing in other ensembles. As a profession, classical music will be become far less attractive than it has been for the past fifty years. (My grandfather was hired as a violinist by the New York Philharmonic in 1934, during the height of the Depression; he was paid well and lived like a king. Those days will be gone forever.) And it isn't just salaries that are threatened. The Minnesota Orchestra settlement, for example, called for almost a 12 percent reduction in the number of full-time musicians, from ninety-five to eighty-four. Other boards are likely to press for similar reductions in orchestra size, and unions will be forced to accept these terms or see their orchestras close. This "nuclear option" will essentially nullify the power of unions.

For a majority of regional ensembles, management's search for "sustainability" is likely to be viewed through a single lens, focusing only on cost reduction (not revenue enhancement). Per service contracts and smaller budgets will lead to less exciting performance programs and more modest education programs, with less overall quality than that of a more stable ensemble. As a result, the number of donors willing to sustain such organizations will fall. As online music delivery improves and technology that can recreate concert-hall sound is perfected, there will be even less demand for live performances by regional orchestras. Fewer performances will reduce opportunities both for earned income and for contributions. And as contributions and earned income fall, orchestra management will require even fewer services from musicians. Without a major educational program to develop new audiences, the demand for performances is likely to fall even further. This downward spiral will continue until many orchestras simply shrink into irrelevance.

The Nashville Symphony Orchestra struggled to make the payments on a loan for construction of its Schermerhorn Symphony Center. The 110-year-old Honolulu Symphony shut down in 2010 because of financial and management problems. Symphonies in New Mexico, Minnesota, and Utah — as well as in Syracuse, Louisville, Detroit, Philadelphia, and Charlotte — have all faced significant financial problems. In early 2014, the Memphis Symphony announced that, unless it can raise a substantial new endowment, it will cease to be a significant regional orchestra. The symphony is not bankrupt; however, its board recognizes that it simply cannot continue to operate as in the past. Expect similar announcements through the coming decades.

With fewer regional orchestras to offer career-building opportunities to young performers, the number of world-class conductors and soloists will dwindle. And existing organizations such as Young Concert Artists, which provide experience and exposure for young soloists, will have a harder time attracting attention. Perhaps shows like *America's Got Talent* or *American Idol* will provide a model for classical music. One can imagine a similar competition — broadcast nationally or internationally—providing a faster route to stardom (among those who still care about classical music) than the traditional opportunities for career development.

There will still be classical music, of course. The music of Beethoven and Brahms will never completely disappear. While overall interest in classical music may diminish, there will still be many people who want to participate in making music, and even more who will want to listen to it. But the orchestral infrastructure built during the twentieth century is going to be dismantled, to a large extent, in the twenty-first.

THEATER IN 2035

Theater organizations should fare better than symphony orchestras. Demand for theater performances is far higher than that for classical music, perhaps because theater tells stories, perhaps because it is a more visual art form, perhaps because it feels more relevant to many audience members.

The for-profit theater industry should thrive, as the number of movie and television stars anxious to participate in Broadway productions has increased dramatically. Such performers can earn significant salaries as well as the prestige now associated with starring in a Broadway show. The stars drive up the ticket prices (and the ticket prices attract the stars). The profit potential of a hit show is now very large. Among recent shows, *The Book of Mormon*, *Wicked*, *The Phantom of the Opera*, and *The Lion King* have all returned astronomical amounts to their producers. This has encouraged additional investment in for-profit theater. It also has encouraged regional companies to attempt to move their shows to Broadway. After some dismal years in the 1970s, we now have more shows looking for theaters than we have theaters. (But this phenomenon has been restricted to New York and does not necessarily extend to for-profit theaters in other cities.) As Broadway shows grow more and more popular, featuring higher production values and more stars, we should expect that they will be broadcast, for a price, to people's homes. Stephen Sondheim's *Merrily We Roll Along* has already been broadcast from London's Menier Chocolate Factory to

American movie screens. Many more such broadcasts will certainly follow.

But today's array of not-for-profit theater companies is likely to shrink, as marginal organizations will find it hard to compete with big for-profit productions and with other forms of storytelling.

We are already witnessing the division of regional theater into two groups: those that regularly send productions to Broadway — such as Harvard's American Repertory Theater, the La Jolla Playhouse, and the Steppenwolf Theatre Company — and those that don't. While these successes often represent additional revenue for regional theaters, they also provide an important boost in prestige — which can attract larger donations.

Those theater organizations that consistently produce interesting work will become important providers of content for other media, just as hit Broadway musicals have been important providers of content for the movie industry. (And as regional theaters gain the capacity to broadcast from their home bases, the pressure to move a show to Broadway may be lessened.) But success will become increasingly difficult for small theater organizations; the focus will be on large-scale productions rather than small, intimate, or avant-garde work.

More people will experience "theater" in their homes. Ironically, this stay-at-home trend will follow several decades of building larger arts venues. Beginning with the opening of Lincoln Center in the mid-1960s, planners have touted arts centers as a means of revitalizing cities, creating vibrant hubs of activity, and attracting visitors and tourists. The fact that donors were happy to provide the resources for construction often made the opportunity too good to pass up. Politicians encouraged the development of arts centers and arts organizations eagerly anticipated the drawing power of new venues. But these facilities were conceived and developed at a time when almost no one anticipated the online distribution of arts events. While there will certainly be some live performances in the future, there will most likely be fewer of them, with these clustered in major cities. It is not clear what types of activity will fill the hundreds of venues constructed over the past twenty years, as many of the surviving companies will be too small to afford the costs of performing in a large theater. (In the Washington, D.C., area alone, a host of theaters were constructed over the past decade.)

In fact, many arts organizations are already feeling "house poor." New facilities are almost invariably larger than their predecessors—and more expensive to operate. When a growing percentage of an organization's budget is allocated to paying for a facility, less will be devoted to programming and marketing, the two real income generators. With less art, less marketing, and higher overhead, it is not surprising that many arts institutions are experiencing difficulties with cash flow. Although many boards have been searching for new and creative ways to use their facilities (thus generating new streams of revenue), these efforts have been mostly in vain. With fewer organizations offering performances in the future, and most of these producing fewer events than they do now, the occupancy rate of many arts centers is going to decline. Because many of these structures were purpose-built and won't easily be converted to other uses, we are going to have an ever-growing number of white elephants. A few arts centers will remain major players, hosting world-class organizations, attracting large donor bases, and serving as broadcast headquarters. But many others will sit vacant, reminders of a different era, not unlike the Colosseum in Rome and the Parthenon in Athens.

OPERA: A NEW PARADIGM

As in theater, there will be stark differences between national and regional opera companies. Regional companies will face reduced demand, owing to the in-home broadcasts that will become a natural outgrowth of movie-theater opera. The difference in price between electronically distributed opera and regional opera will grow wider, as will the difference in quality. As the costs of hiring singers, stagehands, and orchestral musicians rise, there will undoubtedly be efforts to reduce salaries. (Unlike other industries, the arts experience no improvement in productivity to offset the inflation in costs.) Stagehand salaries can be extraordinarily high; one stagehand at Carnegie Hall made over $450,000 in 2012 and several others earned nearly as much! While stagehands provide a much-needed service, such salaries are not likely to be supportable in the future, even by the very largest of organizations. How can an organization justify asking its musicians to accept salary reductions while leaving other pay scales untouched?

The quality of performances by regional opera companies will not keep pace with that of the national companies with access to the biggest stars, best conductors, and most lavish sets and costumes. While differences in quality are evident today (and have been since the advent of regional opera), most people do not have regular access to live, in-person performances at the handful of major companies across the nation and around the world. In the future, broadcast performances by these great companies will be accessible, on demand, to everyone. One will have the same access to companies from New York City as to companies from London or Moscow. (However, we do expect to see far fewer European opera houses in total. Government ministries are already encouraging mergers in an effort to conserve resources. As funding is cut, some companies simply will not survive. In Italy, for example, only three opera houses are currently solvent. A shakeout is certain to occur, resulting in an ugly period of retrenchment featuring numerous strikes, outbursts by the press, and political maneuvering.)

As online broadcasts make comparing the quality of performances much easier, one would expect the demand for performances by smaller regional companies to fall. Further improvements in technology—allowing special effects or sound enhancement not possible in the opera house itself—may place regional companies at an even greater disadvantage.

The difference in demand also will put downward pressure on the ticket prices charged by regional companies. If the artists and production quality are not comparable with those of national companies, it will be difficult to charge prices that are commensurate with costs. As the current group of opera donors begins to die off—and as large national companies expand the reach of their fund-raising efforts—income will again decrease. It is likely that the number of regional opera companies will fall; most of those that do survive will produce less opera each season.

National companies also will struggle to balance their budgets, since producing opera will remain expensive and there will be competition with other arts organizations for donors and audience members who can afford very high ticket prices. But these larger groups will have opportunities for added revenue from the electronic distribution of their performances and access to a national (or international) pool of donors. Of course, as the number of organizations broadcasting their performances increases, the competition for viewers also will increase. While the Metropolitan Opera had a virtual monopoly when it began its broadcasts, the field is growing rapidly. This will place pressure on the prices charged for broadcast performances, which will further hurt the regionals (since their ticket prices will seem comparatively higher), while reducing the profitability of the large companies. Not all of them will survive either. If electronic distribution is implemented properly, however, it can help build a national, or even international, donor base. The impact of electronic distribution on fund-raising can only grow; in the future, it is likely to be required of all major arts organizations. Executives will need to become expert in the operation and financing of such broadcasts, as well as the cultivation of donors from a distance, further increasing the sophistication required to be a successful arts manager.

The Kennedy Center, for example, already raises two-thirds of its contributions (some $50 million of the $75 million raised annually) outside of the Washington, D.C., area. Some of these funds are contributed by a committee of arts patrons who come from many different countries. Imagine how much more could be raised—and how much larger that international committee could grow—when Kennedy Center programming is accessible to hundreds of millions of people across the globe, and when those with real interest are cultivated properly, with subtle (or not-so-subtle) fund-raising pitches.

One can imagine the "exclusive" benefits offered to people who want to feel closer to the Kennedy Center: "private" backstage tours, views of an opera rehearsal, or invitations to a taping (all conducted online, of course). But there will be competition with other large institutions — the Metropolitan Opera, the Royal Opera House, and the Paris Opera, for example — all of whom will be vying for attention. The ability to implement marketing and fund-raising campaigns effectively (especially in terms of donor cultivation and stewardship) will be a crucial factor in achieving fiscal stability in this high-budget, high-stakes environment. Because American arts institutions currently have far more experience in these areas than their European counterparts, they are likely to have the initial competitive advantage.

Broadcasting also will provide a way to engage younger audiences. The Metropolitan Opera and other organizations have already begun to offer abridged performances for children, although these now reach only a relatively small audience, often at a very high price. In the future, expect to witness alliances between arts organizations and school systems to provide arts education via the Internet. Current online portals, such as the Kennedy Center's ArtsEdge.com (which supplies information for teachers and activities for students), are likely to expand their capabilities in the future as school systems and universities seek ways to lower costs. Online recreational arts programs also will become more popular as parents seek arts experiences for their children at a reasonable price. Creating and viewing art is fun and rewarding; no amount of social or economic change will alter that basic fact. The sites that offer the best of these programs will begin to build a group of young people with allegiance to their organizations. If five-year-olds get used to visiting the Web site of the Royal Opera House, for example, and enjoy the games, activities, and performances available there, they are likely to feel closer to this institution than to any local opera company.

The overall reduction in the number of opera companies will make it correspondingly difficult to become an opera singer, concert artist, or conductor. Those who do find employment will face additional hurdles to becoming a star, since the amount of serious criticism will be vastly reduced, as will the network of regional companies that can help young artists build their careers. The most talented — and most fortunate — artists will be recognized early in their careers and engaged by the major opera houses; the remainder will have far fewer performing opportunities. Because sales of future broadcasts will rest, in part, on the fame of singers, directors, and conductors, the large opera companies and symphonies will have an incentive to invest in promoting talent, not unlike record companies in the past.

Artists and their managers will have to play larger roles in building celebrity. This is already a trend. Today's managers often develop important, visible projects for their artists. Despite this change, managers have lost a substantial portion of their traditional clout, as the number of truly famous artists has declined and the fees they can demand are falling. The days in which a major agent could pressure (if not blackmail) a large opera company to engage his singers are virtually over. If the cash-strapped opera companies of the future urge artists to further reduce their fees, then managers will come under corresponding pressure to reduce the amounts that they charge artists. As all organizations strive for reduced costs, it would not be surprising to see the manager function assumed by the arts institutions themselves. In the 1950s, movie studios created stables of famous artists who became "their" stars; similarly, we can expect major opera houses to hoard the singers who bring them high ratings and high visibility.

As broadcasts become more common, it is likely that the qualities that define an opera star will be determined less by the way the voice projects in an opera house and more by appearance, acting ability, and charisma. Just as the performers who were successful in silent movies could not necessarily make the transition to talkies, and those actors who made careers in radio did not necessarily become television stars, performers who have been successful in opera houses may not necessarily "sell" on screen. The experience of listening to an opera in person is likely to be very different from watching it on a screen. And the audio enhancement that will be available in a broadcast should be able to conceal a multitude of vocal sins. Some opera singers with beautiful but relatively small voices already are able to achieve remarkable success in recordings. In the future, we should expect that some singers who have become huge stars on broadcasts will disappoint when heard in person.

The profitability of online ventures will be determined, to a large extent, by the fees that can be charged by artists and others associated with the production. As broadcasts become more popular, all of the participants—from the lead singers to the chorus, from the orchestra to the stagehands—will demand higher salaries. Some television stars now earn millions of dollars per episode; opera stars will only be able to raise their salaries if they can regularly draw a substantial audience to their broadcasts. Those organizations unwilling to pay will lose the biggest stars to other opera houses. In the past, singers' fees were bid up by international opera houses that received large government subsidies; now the major competitors will be those with the largest online presence.

Unless substantial underwriting can be attracted, the price that opera companies can charge for these broadcasts will be the second determinant of profitability. There are likely to be fees for each broadcast, or for a subscription series, just as there already is when renting a movie through Netflix or purchasing a pay-per-view boxing match. These prices will likely be tiered: big events with huge stars will have different prices than more modest attractions. As the required technology becomes cheaper, and the number of institutions offering broadcasts increases, prices are likely to fall. Although most arts institutions will need broadcasts to attract audiences and donors, they may not end up being as profitable as anticipated.

Online broadcasts, of course, can easily cross national boundaries; Metropolitan Opera movie-theater broadcasts, for example, already go to dozens of countries. While opera companies will be competing for the services of singers, conductors, and designers, opera consumers will be able to select among different productions, choosing those that best match their tastes. Viewers will be able to choose between *La Traviata* at the Metropolitan Opera, *Aida* at the Royal Opera House, or *Eugene Onegin* from the Bolshoi. There will come a time when many different broadcasts of *La Bohème* are available, just as there already are many different recordings of that opera. Consumers will choose the one they wish to see the most. It is a tantalizing prospect from the audience's perspective, but a scary one from the viewpoint of the opera houses themselves. One cannot be certain that, as supply increases, demand will as well. While movie-theater viewership of opera broadcasts has increased, the vast majority of attendees identify themselves as frequent opera-goers. It is not clear that electronic distribution is producing a new generation of opera lovers, as advertised. As opera houses face increasing competition for viewership, this may serve to lower ticket prices and force organizations to raise production values, include more stars, and offer more promotional gimmicks.

In any event, such a scenario is consistent with the way all industries evolve. A specialty product becomes commoditized, prices fall, and the pressure on profitability becomes more intense. This process can be fast—as it was in the case of transistors—or slow. In a situation where there are multiple providers, the price sensitivity of customers forces prices down. The problem for the arts is that they seldom have been profitable (owing to the productivity problem), so there is no financial cushion if prices begin to fall. To survive a reduction in income from ticket sales, arts institutions must raise additional income from donations or go out of business.

EVOLUTION OF THE DANCE WORLD

From the outside, the dance world will appear to be the least changed of the performing arts genres in the future. The major international companies in Moscow, St. Petersburg, London, Copenhagen, Paris, San Francisco, and New York will be complemented by a few other companies that can create donor bases large enough to sustain themselves. A central challenge for ballet companies will be creating new repertory that can attract an audience of younger people who are not wed to the classics and do not discriminate among ballet, contemporary dance, and popular dance quite like their parents do. It is difficult to name one work that has entered the standard repertory of ballet companies in the past thirty years. A majority of tickets are still sold for a handful of full-length ballets—

including *Swan Lake, Sleeping Beauty, Giselle, The Nutcracker, Romeo and Juliet, La Bayadère,* and *Coppélia*—and a group of shorter works by Balanchine, Robbins, Ashton, Tharp, Kylián, and a few others. Will an art form that has been essentially stagnant be able to compete for audiences in a world of high-tech wizardry?

When audience members are watching ballet in their homes (and recording their favorite performances), it will be difficult to get them to purchase new performances of the same works. This problem befell the classical music industry when CDs replaced LPs; since CDs didn't scratch or break, customers purchased their favorite performances of specific works, then stopped purchasing more. Some consumers would want to hear a familiar work performed by a new phenom, but such buyers were in the minority, leading to huge problems in the recording industry. Unless a group of choreographers can create new works that attract new audiences, the ballet world will face a substantial challenge in the future.

In modern dance, a handful of major organizations will survive, at best. Even now there are only a select few, including the Alvin Ailey organization, which has built unparalleled support for an organization of color. From its start in 1958, the Ailey company has had the benefit of multiple choreographers. When Alvin Ailey passed away, it was therefore natural for the dancers and the audience to experience new works in the repertory. And in *Revelations*, the company has a perennial favorite that maintains its audience. But will audiences continue to support the organization just to see *Revelations* for another twenty years?

The mid-sized companies with a single choreographer (many of them modern dance legends) are likely to shrink or disappear entirely. The Martha Graham Dance Company, for example, is already a smaller version of its former self, while the Merce Cunningham Dance Company was folded in a most orderly fashion, according to the wishes of Cunningham himself. Twyla Tharp does not maintain a permanent company anymore, and Paul Taylor would be 105 years old in 2035! With no new organizations growing and building support, it is unclear if we will have the marquee companies to replace the institutions created by these legends.

Modern dance is most vital when a group of choreographers are creating new works that entice new viewers, often the younger people that other art forms strive to attract. Despite the presence of many dynamic younger choreographers, no current organization has captured the imagination of audiences and tour presenters, and none is poised to replace the senior companies. Mark Morris started the most successful recent company, and he will be nearing eighty by 2035. Will he still be producing new work? Will his company still exist? Without a few modern dance stars, the entire field will suffer. As less money is invested in the art form, modern dance may evaporate from view, especially as the larger ballet companies add modern choreography to their repertoires.

Many of the mid-sized regional ballet companies also are likely to shrink or disappear. Companies in Miami, Philadelphia, Oakland, San Jose, Orlando, and elsewhere already have experienced major crises. Although some of these organizations may build a level of support that allows them to maintain operations, it is doubtful that they will all survive.

One ominous trend may spell doom for many regional ballet companies: the decline of *Nutcracker* sales. This perennial Christmas favorite has been a financial mainstay, with many companies depending on *Nutcracker* sales to support the remainder of their seasons. As this holiday tradition becomes more expensive — and as alternative forms of entertainment become more attractive — many families are choosing to forego their annual *Nutcracker* attendance. Ballet needs new repertory that will encourage its audience members to buy tickets; this will be especially important if *Nutcracker* sales continue to decline and the remainder of the ballet season must begin to carry its own weight.

Almost every sizeable dance company requires some level of touring to sustain itself, as there is not enough demand in most cities to support full-time work. Of the major American ballet companies, for example, only a few have built long seasons in their home cities, allowing them to guarantee weeks of work for their dancers and forego most touring opportunities. Dance requires consistent performance and rehearsal to maintain quality levels. That need to perform, coupled with the lack of demand in any one city, is the reason so many dance companies tour.

In the future, successful dance companies will be those—like the Alvin Ailey American Dance Theater—that build strong touring programs or online broadcasts that earn high fees. If a few major ensembles tour or broadcast extensively, they may effectively replace the local companies that are unable to perform at the same high level. The competition faced by local companies will be particularly strong if demand falls. One can imagine a cadre of ten or so major ballet companies serving the dance needs of the entire country.

While this may turn out to be efficient, that reduction in the number of dance organizations will come at a price. Each company has an opportunity, through the activities of its artistic leadership, to create important, innovative, and exciting work that moves the field. When one reduces the number of organizations of a specific genre, one reduces the odds of the next great work being created. The most interesting works are not always created by the largest companies, even though they are the ones most likely to survive a shakeout. Some large institutions will be disinclined to take the huge risks necessary to allow the art form to develop.

Dance institutions, like most arts organizations, do more than simply offer performances. They provide a myriad of services to the community: from arts programs in the public schools, to ballet classes for young children and lectures and demonstrations for adults. When the number of local organizations is reduced, the amount of community outreach also falls and the probability of bringing new people into the art form similarly diminishes. This will further reduce demand, lowering both attendance and donations, and thereby creating additional problems for the field.

A reduction in the number of companies also means fewer opportunities for artists to find work. Our conservatories and dance schools already produce far more artists than can find employment. While it is wonderful that so many young people get the chance to pursue their dreams, it is also a sad fact of life that many will leave college, burdened by debt, with little hope of earning enough to support a family. Graduates in many industries are facing the same challenge, of course, but artists face the longest odds. Salaries in the arts are already falling, the number of job possibilities are few and far between, and demand for their services is likely to be further reduced in the future. Arts students also are least likely to be able to pursue their college degrees online. While academic courses will become more available (and less costly) via the Internet, it is unlikely that in-person instruction in singing, dancing, acting, or composing will ever be satisfactorily replaced by online classes. Artists will therefore have the unfortunate combination of an expensive education with few opportunities for employment.

A FUND-RAISING EXPLOSION

Major arts organizations will increasingly need to become fund-raising machines. While some people say that arts institutions already have begun to overemphasize fund-raising at the expense of art-making, the need to increase contributions dramatically will force all arts organizations to intensify their development efforts. As the competition for revenue grows, the organizations with the best art, strongest boards, and best-organized fund-raising efforts will attract donors at the expense of others. The largest arts organizations—those with international stature and popular online broadcasts—will be able to offer unparalleled visibility to their most generous donors. Instead of announcing sponsorships to the few thousand people who read a theater program, or the tens of thousands who receive promotional materials (but may not read them), online announcements could reach hundreds of thousands or even millions of people across the globe. For those sponsors seeking visibility, this increases their return dramatically. Institutions of more modest size will suffer simply because they will not be able to compete on a level with the largest organizations.

Not unlike television advertising today, the attractiveness of such sponsorships to corporations, foundations, or individuals will depend on the ability of the arts organization to attract large numbers of viewers to their online programming. One can imagine the remarkable pressure that might be placed on the programmers at major opera companies, for example, by those with responsibility for financial results. "Do we have to produce *Lulu* this season? Can't we do *Barber of Seville*, instead? It's far more popular." And with professional critics losing clout, there will be far less external pressure for programming that is important and daring. In fact, it will be fair to question whether the largest opera companies are functioning more like for-profit entertainment companies than old-fashioned non-profits. This charge has already been directed at some New York theater companies whose work regularly competes for Tony Awards with for-profit productions. If these organizations are developing work for the mass market, are they really occupying a different space than the for-profit producers? And should they really be able to offer tax deductions to their donors? As more arts organizations depend on broadcasts to cover their costs of production, these questions will be asked with greater frequency. And considering the federal government's ongoing quest to reduce its budget deficit, the fate of tax deductibility for contributions may rest on the answers.

The shift to online broadcasts will create other convergences with the for-profit entertainment industry. For example, it is likely that arts awards will change both in scope and impact. Currently, awards are offered for local productions—in New York, for instance, or Chicago, or London. In the not-so-distant future, as more productions are available for viewing online and geography no longer prohibits judges from evaluating distant productions, some group is likely to offer awards for excellence in a genre, unrelated to location. The competition for these awards will be fierce, just as they are currently for the Oscars, Tonys, BAFTAs, and others. Winning the award for best opera, best concert, or best ballet will offer an important seal of approval, creating audience demand for future Webcasts and attracting sponsors who want to be associated with the best. One can easily imagine the gala presentation of the International Arts Awards, held in London or Paris or Beijing or New York—and available for viewing online, of course. The evening will feature an unprecedented gathering of arts luminaries; most of the serious arts production in the world will cease for a day or two as the best and most famous gather for this remarkably visible event. Will these awards be decided by a blue-ribbon panel or will the public vote for their favorites? Online voting from millions of fans could trigger widespread campaigns for the nominated productions.

Winning such an award will help attract donors and, importantly, board members as well. The larger arts organizations will have to intensify their search for the most potent board members. As the need for large contributions grows, only the most generous patrons—with access to other like-minded contributors—will be considered satisfactory board members. Board members will be expected to make very large gifts annually and to solicit others who can do the same. As these have not been traditional roles for board members at foreign arts institutions, American organizations will have to convince foreign board members that their roles extend to giving and getting funds.

And there is little doubt that board membership for large organizations will become increasingly international, as fund-raising activities expand over larger geographical territories. The Kennedy Center established its international committee in 2002 to raise funds for international presentations. By 2035, it is likely that international representatives will serve not only on special committees, but also on boards with fiduciary responsibility. Only those organizations that serve an international market—and achieve international acclaim—will be able to attract the most generous of this new breed of board member.

Today, board members at most arts organizations in other regions of the world are only modestly helpful as donors, with very few feeling an obligation either to give or solicit funds. Traditionally, such boards have been viewed as overseers of government resources. In many cases, board members were appointed by the governments themselves. Boards would approve strategic decisions, annual budgets, and performing calendars, but would not involve themselves in resource-gathering to the same extent as their American counterparts. Arts boards in other countries also were typically smaller than U.S. boards, since the oversight role did not require as many governors. In fact, numerous arts organizations maintained a separate fund-raising entity, such as a trust, with its own, separate board. In these cases, the trust would be responsible for overseeing the endowment and raising any private funds. For example, my board at the Royal Opera House was appointed by the Secretary of State for Culture, Media, and Sport; there were seven people on the board and only one made a substantial financial contribution, even though the organization was conducting a capital campaign. A separate Royal Opera House Trust endeavored to raise the necessary operating and capital funds. But the boards of the two organizations often clashed, making it difficult at best to implement a coherent fund-raising strategy.

It is possible that American arts organizations will help create cultures of philanthropy in other countries. Many large foreign arts organizations—including the Louvre, the Royal Shakespeare Company, the Budapest Festival Orchestra, and the Mariinsky Theater—currently raise money in the United States (through U.S.-based charities). In the future, American arts organizations will be appealing to wealthy donors in other countries. To the extent that these efforts are successful, with adequate stewardship of the resulting relationships, we will be teaching foreign patrons that arts sponsorship can be fun and enriching. This could encourage such patrons to support the work of local arts institutions and give those institutions a model for mounting strong development efforts as well, helping them to build private sources of funding to replace dwindling government support.

As international arts organizations become more reliant on contributed funds, they also will seek to attract strong board members. Although European arts organizations may not admire the American system of arts funding, they remain jealous of the generosity of American board members. As European organizations turn increasingly to private fund-raising, they will find themselves on a collision course with American institutions. Such competition won't be entirely new, since many international arts organizations already have established fund-raising operations to mine the philanthropic culture of the United States. Over time, however, the search for new donors is likely to move overseas, with American fund-raisers combing Europe, Asia, and South America for the wealthiest arts lovers.

We have lived through the golden age of regional arts organizations, with numerous opportunities to build expertise and gain employment. By 2035, much of this system will be dismantled and there will be fewer opportunities for artists to find work. Our conservatories and arts schools will be challenged to attract enough students to cover their overheads; many will close. Similar cutbacks in Europe will affect young American artists who traditionally looked overseas for experience. Young opera singers, for example, often moved to Europe during the early part of their careers, since provincial opera houses throughout the continent were happy to hire well-trained American singers at modest fees. Renée Fleming, for instance, performed in Europe before coming to the world's attention. But as government cutbacks force companies either to reduce their performing schedules or close entirely, these opportunities also will become scarce.

THE NEW MUSEUM

While the outlook for the performing arts is dire, museums have better chances for survival. New technology has made museum visits more exciting, and looking at a great painting or sculpture on a screen does not duplicate the in-person experience. While many will say this is true of the performing arts as well, the cost per visit is much greater for the performing arts than for museums. That discrepancy will encourage many to watch opera, ballet, or theater at home while continuing to make trips to the local museum. Much concern was expressed when New York's Museum of Modern Art raised its entry fee to twenty-five dollars, even though this is a small fraction of the cost of one performance at the Metropolitan Opera. But MOMA has not suffered from its increased fee; in fact, it is about to expand again. Other museums will undoubtedly increase their entry fees as well. It will be interesting to see when the reduction in attendance will occur, as high fees must eventually encourage people to embrace online forms of distribution. If museums are not careful, they could experience the same drop in demand as the performing arts.

No matter how the viewing of art is distributed, however, museums will retain a most critical function: safeguarding and conserving collections of immense value. And then there is their other, less visible role: as purchase advisors for wealthy patrons. With so much interest in contemporary art today, and so much money at stake, curators have become the unofficial advisors to art collectors who, in turn, support the institutions that engage the curators. This situation is unlikely to change soon, although some of the very wealthiest of arts patrons are now hiring their own curators and building their own museums.

Because convenience will remain a factor in determining how people view art, some will choose to watch from home. But it is hard to imagine that those living near major museums or traveling to their host cities will not continue to pay in-person visits.

As in the performing arts, it will be the large institutions — such as the Museum of Modern Art, the Hermitage, and the British Museum — that will embrace the new technologies, mount the public programming, and implement the marketing campaigns that build visitorship, a broad base of donors, and strong boards. The biggest prizes — gifts of important collection items — will go increasingly to those institutions that have the staff to cater to the needs of donors, and the stability to assure those donors that their gifts will be cared for in perpetuity.

The building boom of the past three decades is likely to be over, as fewer museums will have the resources to build new galleries in the future. The exceptions to this trend will be for buildings financed by individuals to house their own collections, either at single-collector museums like the Broad Museum in Los Angeles, or in galleries attached to existing institutions. At most museums, however, physical growth will be constrained by the loss of older donors who were willing to give huge gifts for capital expansion (and whose children have different giving priorities).

DECLINING DIVERSITY

While both the performing and visual arts will be changing in the future, it is the diversity within each art form that will change the most. As financial strength, artistic resources, audience base, and board potency become concentrated in just a few organizations, one can be certain that these will be mainstream institutions — the ones that traditionally serve higher-income arts audiences. While minorities as a group may comprise a majority of Americans in the near future, the majority of the wealth will continue to belong to white people, and the donor base will reflect this fact. Organizations that provide art which emerges from specific ethnic communities or that serve those communities will be relegated to the minor leagues. This is not a new trend. Apart from the Alvin Ailey American Dance Theater, it is nearly impossible to name an organization of color with an annual budget of more than $10 million. The distribution of wealth in the United States is mirrored in the distribution of the arts.

Theaters of color are in disarray. Of the many potent African American theater companies formed in the second half of the twentieth century, most have either gotten smaller or have disappeared entirely. Crossroads Theater, for example, was once a thriving company in New Brunswick, New Jersey. After winning a regional Tony Award in 1999, it suffered through a near-death experience and is now a shadow of its former self. Of the several promising Latino theater companies, such as Pregones Theater in New York City, none has yet earned a national reputation for excellence.

Dance companies of color are experiencing the same fate as their white counterparts — as their founders age or die, they cannot maintain their vibrancy. Company founders often put their hearts, souls, and cash into these enterprises. With their passing, a new generation of leaders has been unable to assure the survival of their organizations.

As dedicated as these founders were, they rarely were able to build support beyond the major foundations and government agencies in their cities. And though their boards were passionate, they were not potent. Many boards of such organizations function more as community groups than as fund-raising entities. The members are passionate about the work of the organization and the importance of the arts in their communities but have neither the personal resources to contribute large sums nor connections to others of great means. This has severely limited the size and reach of most arts organizations of color.

By 2035, it is doubtful that many of the currently existing organizations of color will be thriving. This has important implications for the accessibility of live, in-person performing arts for everyone except well-to-do people in major cities. It is likely that only a very small elite will have ready access to high-quality arts *in person*. This will further disenfranchise the people who suspect that the arts are not for them. It is possible that the arts will come to mean something reserved only for the wealthy, like yachts or equestrian sports.

Although new organizations will undoubtedly be formed to meet the needs of communities of color, it is not likely that any will achieve success on a large scale, unless a potent group of board members can attract a staff leader of true vision and skill. It has become increasingly difficult for smaller arts organizations to attract the type of leadership necessary to build great institutions, since larger arts organizations (which pay much higher salaries) siphon off the best talent. Even when a skilled director can be engaged, the lack of local arts journalism makes it challenging for young, exciting groups to establish the reputation for excellence required to build a larger base of support.

ARTS MANAGERS IN A NEW AGE

With the growing divide between larger and smaller organizations, salaries for arts managers will continue to bifurcate. While such salaries have risen across the board, the leaders of the nation's largest arts organizations now command salaries that approach $1 million, while salaries at most other organizations remain under $100,000. Similarly, development directors at larger institutions are now earning several hundred thousand dollars a year; this equates to the total salary budget for many smaller institutions. This chasm is likely to grow in future years.

Arts managers currently face a difficult conundrum: while much of the most interesting art is produced by smaller arts organizations, the larger institutions pay much higher salaries and have the resources to produce arts projects of great magnitude. It can be difficult to resist the temptation to work for a major institution like Carnegie Hall or the San Francisco Opera even if one's own tastes are more eclectic. As more and more students leave school burdened with debt, their job choices are increasingly influenced by salary levels, job security, and retirement benefits.

Nevertheless, many arts managers join the field hoping to engage with an organization where they can work closely with artists, and where the aesthetic of the organization matches their own. After all, one of the great rewards of working in the not-for-profit realm comes from attaching oneself to an organization with a mission similar to one's own. In the for-profit sector, every corporation has essentially the same mission: to reward its shareholders by making as much money as possible for as long as possible. It can be difficult to find passion for such a mission, especially if one is not, personally, a shareholder of the corporation.

In the not-for-profit arts, however, we can work for an organization that is committed to accomplishing what we ourselves find important. This compensates in a big way for the lower salaries in the not-for-profit world. When a small arts institution is thriving, it can feel remarkably rewarding to be part of the team. When such institutions encounter periods of poor cash flow, however, many boards and senior staff members lose sight of the true missions of their organizations and focus instead on balancing the books. This often antagonizes the staff and artists who came to work for the organization only because of the stated mission. These members of the organization may feel cheated if, after all their hard work and sacrifice, that mission is compromised.

This feeling may become especially evident when a board looks to engage a financial expert, often from the corporate sector, rather than a manager with true arts experience. In difficult times, the board may hope that a leader with financial acumen can fix the institution's money problems. While this strategy sometimes works, more often the board has confused someone who can measure the size of the problem (a financial person) with someone who can solve the problem by finding new revenue (an arts entrepreneur). When timely and accurate financial reports continue to tell the same story of cash-flow constraints, board members often learn the error of their logic.

By this time, many of the organization's most dedicated staff members will have left to find a more hospitable place to work. In the industry's current state, experienced arts managers have opportunities to move from organization to organization, building their careers by steadily increasing their responsibilities. This may not be as easy in the future, if there are fewer mid-sized organizations to provide steppingstones for younger arts managers. It is possible that the arts industry may suffer from the same system that now applies to law firms, in which the best graduates of the best schools go to work for the largest institutions, enduring an "up or out" system that roots out under-performers.

The managers who will run our future multi-national arts institutions—the organizations with board members from around the globe and huge electronic distribution networks, audiences, and donor bases—are likely to receive salaries that mimic those of corporate leaders and university presidents. Board members of small, local arts organizations, with their limited budgets, are therefore going to have difficulty attracting the best managerial talent. The pay, benefits, and security at larger organizations will be too tempting for the most talented arts managers to turn down. Since the success of an arts institution is, in large measure, a function of the quality of top management, this "brain drain" will hurt smaller organizations substantially.

Make no mistake: the movement of the most talented managers to the largest organizations is a trend that seriously threatens the fabric of arts organizations in this country. One can separate arts institutions into two groups: those that are managed well, with an entrepreneurial leader in charge, and those that have less effective management. There is nearly a one-to-one correspondence between good management and good organizational health.

Arts organizations with strong management will be able to thrive even when prevailing trends work against them. In the future, too many of our smaller organizations will find that they cannot retain the best managers. Even when such institutions can find effective and ambitious young leaders, these leaders are likely to depart for larger, more established institutions that pay better. Replacing the departing leader will be a huge challenge, as lightning rarely strikes twice in the same place. Even now small organizations that lose a strong leader often find that the new executive is not a satisfactory replacement. This will become even more common in the future, making it far more difficult for smaller arts organizations to grow into larger ones. The sort of leadership that allowed organizations like Glimmerglass Opera or Mark Morris Dance Group to grow into potent institutions will not be attracted by salaries too low to cover the cost of living and the repayment of student loans.

The only real winners in this new world order will be the few celebrity artists and arts managers who benefit from the acclaim that comes from participating in widely distributed productions — along with the consumers who prefer to watch opera on their iPads or in their home theaters. The choices available to these consumers will be spectacular and varied.

Amateurs and hobbyists, of course, will have numerous and exciting opportunities to make art and to share that art with both friends and strangers. But for many others in the art world, the future does not look as bright. Young artists will struggle to be seen or heard, while small organizations will struggle to remain solvent and to pursue their missions with vigor. Audiences in many mid-sized cities will lose their local theater, opera, and ballet companies, along with their symphonies and perhaps even their museums. People of color will likewise lose access to the organizations that provided targeted opportunities both for enjoying and participating in the arts.

The current network of regional institutions, boards, and management teams will begin to unravel. And the competition among the largest institutions — for artists, ratings, donors, and board members — will become far more intense.

The notion that "all arts are local" will become simply a memory.

BRAVE NEW WORLD,

. . . .

PART II

. . . .

HOW INDUSTRIES EVOLVE

Where do these projections come from? Is this simply a matter of conjecture? An educated guess? Am I simply getting pessimistic with age?

In truth, industries evolve in predictable ways, as noted in previous chapters. They may differ with respect to the pace of change, but they typically start and end in the same places. Typically one or more inventors have an idea, let's say to create a vehicle that can take individuals from place to place on their own schedule and at their own pace: the automobile.

When people learn about the product and deem it useful, they begin to buy it. There are typically just a few customers willing to take a risk on the new item, especially if it is technologically advanced. And to begin with, the inventor or manufacturer typically does not have enough capacity to meet a high level of demand. Because relatively few items are being produced, the costs of production are high and not all customers can afford the product.

When other manufacturers realize that the product is worthwhile — and that there is more demand for the product than the inventor can meet — they enter the field as well. In an effort to attract customers away from the initial manufacturer (who has already established some brand recognition), these new manufacturers typically add more features to the product than originally available: new color choices, for example, or power steering, leather seats, and air conditioning. Customers now begin to shop for the product by choosing the features that matter most to them among one or another of the competitors' offerings. (Those of us old enough to remember the VCR will recall that there were two competing technologies: Betamax and VHS. When VHS "won" the battle for consumers, Betamax virtually disappeared.) Through customers' buying choices, manufacturers learn which features are most valued. The first cars, for example, had engines that started with a crank, not a key. Over time, features that consumers once used to differentiate between manufacturers become standard accessories.

As more manufacturers begin to produce the product, its price tends to fall. This occurs not only because competition forces prices down, but also because manufacturers that make more and more of a product learn to do it less expensively. For many products, the price moves quickly downward as demand explodes at new and lower price points. (The manufacturers of semiconductors, for example, saw demand grow very quickly. New and better chips were produced, and costs fell monthly. As prices continued to fall, additional uses for semiconductors were introduced, sales increased, and prices fell even further.) As prices fall and features are added, manufacturers use marketing techniques to explain the new features to potential customers. These actions build the size of the market until an industry is created.

Over time, the specific features that customers truly value are identified and the product becomes more standardized. As this occurs, the choice between manufacturers becomes less important to customers and the product becomes a commodity—relatively indistinguishable from one maker to another. When there is little to distinguish the offering of one competitor from another, customers buy on the basis of price. This is why the Japanese invasion of the automobile market in the 1970s and 1980s was so successful; Japanese manufacturers specialized in producing a good-quality, standardized product at a low cost (in comparison with their American counterparts).

Manufacturers pay a penalty when they fail to realize that customers have settled on a sufficient set of options and become more price-sensitive. In the 1980s, American automobile manufacturers still believed that customers would happily pay a premium for every bell and whistle—but this was a dream world. Prices were higher for American cars, in part because adding different accessories to each automobile, depending on the desires of the particular customer, added substantially to the costs of production. (And the work required to make each American car to the specifications of a particular buyer did not just hurt costs, it hurt quality as well.) As it turned out, however, most American buyers wanted a good, standard car at a low price; they were not willing to pay the extra cost for American-made automobiles. When American manufacturers finally realized this fact, they were forced to make a massive change to their manufacturing capabilities, since producing standardized cars at a low price required far more automation than the traditional manpower-heavy approach. (Hence the loss of manufacturing employment mentioned earlier.)

Of course, there are typically smaller groups of buyers who are looking for more or different features than the norm — and are willing to pay extra for them. These customers create market niches serviced by specialty manufacturers that can demand higher prices. In the automobile market, for example, these customers might want to buy sports cars, SUVs, or high-end luxury vehicles. Unfortunately for American automobile producers, those looking for luxury cars did not find American products attractive either, as these cars looked too much like their lower-end cousins. Such consumers preferred European imports. In this situation, American manufacturers fell in the middle — a classic error of business strategy in which a company is neither efficient enough to produce a product that satisfies those who are price-sensitive, nor skilled enough to produce a product that appeals to niche buyers. Firms that fall in the middle are typically the least profitable in an industry. (Many retailers now find themselves in this predicament — more expensive than Target or Walmart, and not as special as Neiman-Marcus. Their profitability has, not surprisingly, eroded.)

This standard pattern of evolution has been experienced in most industries. And while we in the arts sometimes feel we are different (when I use the term "industry" to describe us in the classes I teach, I frequently get an unpleasant reaction), we truly do act like an industry — even if our mission is not to earn a profit, but to be of service to our communities.

THE PORTER MODEL

Michael Porter, a distinguished professor at the Harvard Business School, defined an industry as having five key participants.

- *Competitors*: those companies that offer similar products to similar customer groups. The level of competition in an industry is dependent, in great measure, on the number of competitors and the similarity of their offerings. When a product has become standardized and there are numerous competitors (in chemicals manufacturing, for example), competition is intense and profits are low, because the only basis of competition is price. When there are few competitors, or when products are very different from each other, manufacturers can charge a premium and profits tend to be easier to come by.

- *Buyers*: those individuals, organizations, or corporations that purchase the offerings of the competitors. When buyers have many choices among similar products, they tend to have more power to force manufacturers to reduce prices. Whether they choose to exercise this power depends, in part, on their price sensitivity—the degree to which they care about price for that product. Price sensitivity is determined both by the price of the object, relative to other purchases, and the "specialness" of the product. People are far more sensitive about the price they pay for rent than for chewing gum, for example. And many are willing to pay a great deal for a Super Bowl ticket because it is so special to them.

- *Suppliers*: the individuals, organizations, or corporations that provide the materials, the venue, and the labor needed to make the product. When there are few suppliers who can provide what is needed, or when, in the case of labor, the suppliers are unionized, the costs of production go up and profitability is squeezed. When supplies are plentiful, it is far easier for an industry to function profitably.

- *New Entrants*: individuals, organizations, or corporations that could enter the field and become competitors in the future. When there are many possible new entrants, it is harder to succeed because future competition is likely to increase. Barriers to entry determine whether new entrants are likely. It is far harder to start an opera company, for instance, than a chamber music ensemble. The amount of time and money required to start a new opera company are formidable barriers. But it is not difficult to start a string quartet; that is why there are so many of them. In the arts, touring represents another form of entry. When it is easy for other arts groups to tour to your region, they can make the field far more competitive. For example, it is relatively easy for modern dance ensembles to tour, since they require neither an orchestra nor a large stage. That is one reason why the Alvin Ailey organization has one of the most robust touring schedules in the arts. The low barrier to entry can make it difficult for local companies to thrive, however, as they can be easily overshadowed by the bigger touring ensembles.

- *Substitute Products*: other products that accomplish something similar to the products of the competitors. When there are numerous substitute products, buyers have more power to force lower prices from competitors, since they can choose to buy substitutes instead. Because so many substitute entertainment products and services have been introduced over the past decade, arts institutions have observed a substantial increase in the power of their buyers. This makes it far harder for them to increase ticket prices as costs rise.

Professor Porter further observes that it is the interactions among these five participants that determine the ease or difficulty of succeeding in an industry. When competitors fight fiercely, when buyers have power to make choices among many similar offerings (or when substitute products are plentiful), and when suppliers have the power to charge higher prices, an industry is going to have its challenges. In the retail industry, for example, so many retailers offer similar goods that competition is high. Because new entrants appear frequently, buyers have a great deal of power. In fact, retailers are pressured to offer discounts even in December, their busiest season. Online shopping, a relatively new substitute, has placed

PORTER MODEL

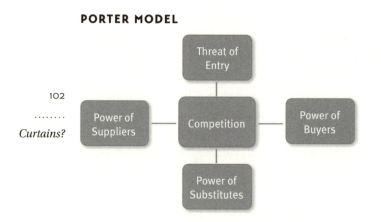

even greater pressure on retail outlets to reduce their prices, since it is so convenient to shop from home. Not surprisingly, retailers are having their profits squeezed.

When a firm creates a new product, buyers are weak because they can only purchase from that one supplier. If it is an attractive product, it will likely outdo substitutes that were created with older technologies. Suppliers have every reason to support the development of this new product since they will have a new market for their own goods and services. And while the threat of new entrants might ultimately be strong, new technologies are typically subject to patent and it often takes some time for others to develop similar offerings. During the period before others enter the industry, profitability can be high.

With the entry of new competitors, who may improve the product by providing more choices to the buyer, things get more difficult for the original inventor. As buyers begin to identify the standard set of features they truly value, the product becomes more of a commodity and buyers get more power. And as prices are bid down, the profitability of the industry is challenged.

I have found this model to be most helpful in describing how an industry is likely to evolve and in predicting the way industry participants will be affected by anticipated changes. Applying it to the arts provides some important insights for the coming decades.

While many of today's arts organizations complain about competition, the truth is that a lack of substantial direct competition has protected the arts for many centuries. Since performances were typically presented live (with the exception of music recordings and television broadcasts), the ballet company or opera company or symphony orchestra in any given city pretty much had the field to its own. Although these organizations did compete with each other (especially with respect to attracting large donors), they could typically find enough support—if they created strong programming and marketed well—to sustain themselves. That is why ticket prices could rise so quickly over the past fifty years. Customers in Omaha who wanted to see an opera had to patronize Opera Omaha; they were relatively powerless to do anything about the ticket price. And while it is true that some cities—such as New York, London, or Paris—were home to a greater number of arts organizations, these places could draw on huge potential audiences.

Until the advent of broadcasts, the arts were truly local. Competition among major opera companies, for example, revolved around guest artists and a few national grants. Collaboration was more helpful than harmful, and there was real incentive for opera and ballet companies to share sets and costumes. When I was running American Ballet Theatre, for instance, we collaborated with the San Francisco Ballet on the creation of *Othello*, a full evening work with choreography by Lar Lubovitch and music by Elliot Goldenthal. ABT performed the work in New York, then the San Francisco Ballet performed the work in their home season. There was no competition and we both benefited from a new production at half the normal cost of creation. When electronic distribution pits the San Francisco Opera against the Lyric Opera of Chicago, however, it is far less likely that they will want to collaborate. Who would get to air the broadcast first? Having a distinctive set of productions will be a big asset in attracting viewers.

Over the past decade, arts organizations have been challenged by a decrease in demand. There have been fewer buyers for subscriptions (due to the aging of our traditional audience), a reduction of interest among younger people (due to a lack of arts education in the schools), and a growing number of substitute products. The

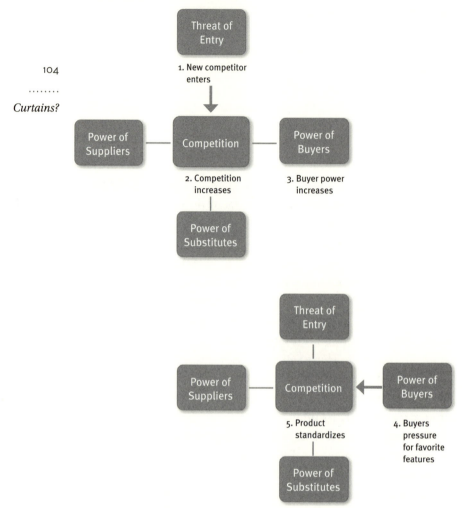

Metropolitan Opera, for example, sells far fewer seats than it did in the relatively recent past. This reduction in demand has given the buyers who do still care about the arts more choice and therefore more power. For many events, it is no longer possible to raise ticket prices to increase income; in some cases, it has been necessary to reduce prices to maintain sales. When the Met tried to raise prices in 2012, ticket sales fell precipitously; in 2014, it was forced to lower

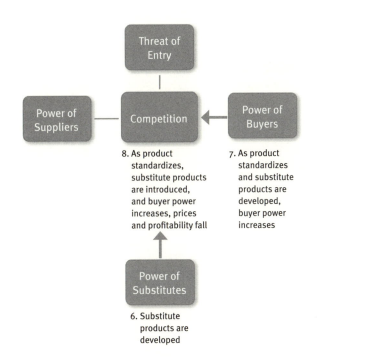

prices. Given this environment, many groups have tried to reduce the costs associated with their principal suppliers (in the case of symphony orchestras, this means musicians). As in Minnesota, one strategy has been to try to force "suppliers" to accept lower salaries by threatening to close if costs do not fall.

In the future, however, we envisage a far higher degree of electronic distribution, to an audience less well educated in the arts. To those of us who have cared about the arts for a long time, electronic distribution seems more like a substitute product than a new competitor. After all, we argue, watching a live performance is simply a different experience than watching the same performance on a movie screen or at home. But to many consumers, especially those young enough to have learned to use an iPad before they learned to speak, the distinctions will not be about those differences in the experience—they will be about comfort, familiarity, expense, and convenience. Why travel to see something one can see at home?

....

Curtains?

Threat of
Entry

1. Broadcasts
introduce
powerful new
competitor

Power of
Suppliers

Competition

Power of
Buyers

2. Competition
increases

3. Buyer power
increases,
forcing price
reduction

Power of
Substitutes

Why plan to be at a theater on a specific day at a specific time when one can watch whenever the mood strikes? And why pay $300 for a ticket when one can watch for $25 on an iPad? For these consumers, electronic distribution represents a substantial new entrant.

Many of us over the age of fifty are happy to travel to a theater, to sit with friends or strangers and share a communal arts experience. But younger people have been trained to sit alone with a set of headphones and to enjoy their entertainment in solitude. They may happily communicate with friends about their experiences, but their idea of sharing is to tweet in real time, not to sit and watch together. One day these young people will be parents and grandparents; like them, future generations will expect entertainment on demand and on a personal device. At home, my generation could only choose between television shows. In the future, people will choose among shows, movies, operas, and concerts — or to play games, read books, or share on social media. The range of choices will only increase as new technologies make watching at home more and more attractive — soon directional sound systems will make headsets obsolete. Those of us who do not appreciate this fundamental difference in the mindsets of younger Americans are in the same danger as those who once disparaged the attractions of "talking pictures."

This represents only a general analysis of the evolution of the arts industry, of course. Discussions of buyers, suppliers, competitors, substitutes, and new entrants are more helpful when the subgroups in each of the five industry participants are identified and analyzed separately. Ballet audiences in New York City are different from operagoers in Omaha, for example, and there are differing substitute products for museums than for theater companies.

THE INCREASING POWER OF DONORS

One important subgroup of buyers demands a separate analysis. This segment is composed of those who purchase access to special events, membership benefits, and so on—the donors. And, yes, donors are buyers. They are purchasing something from the arts organization—perhaps prestige, or access to artists, or an interesting social life. No matter what the motivation, however, donors pay the institution to receive a benefit in return. It is often a different benefit than audience members want but it is a benefit nonetheless.

With the addition of new competitors to the arts industry, donors have seen their power increase. They can choose which arts organizations they wish to support from among many options. And they can demand substantial returns from the organizations they select, in the form of special services and privileges. Although the development operations of arts institutions used to be about asking for money, they are now more about donor services—stewarding the relationship with donors and providing them with rewarding experiences (so they might give more in the future). In fact, the need for contributed dollars is so great that strategy has shifted from soliciting many new donors at a modest level to getting our most potent donors to give more. It is not uncommon to read about gifts of $1 million, $10 million, or even $100 million. This was not the case fifty years ago.

This trend has been enhanced by the rise of the super-wealthy, who can give remarkable sums. The arts organizations that now raise the most money are typically those that offer the best and most customized service. It is not unusual for donors to receive invitations to special events, backstage tours for friends and family, meals with the leadership of the institution, advance notice of programming, meetings with artists (memorialized with photos, suitable for framing), flowers on their birthdays, and valet parking.

Unfortunately for arts organizations, many of the most generous donors are characterized by advanced age. It is a sad fact that younger people are not replacing their parents as major donors as often as arts organizations desire or require. In the past, new donors replaced older ones with regularity — that is why total donations to the arts continued to rise from decade to decade.

To be sure, the average arts patron has always been above middle age. Younger people would be busy building careers and forming families, and often had little discretionary money or time. But as their careers flourished, and their children left the nest, they often found themselves with both time and resources to spare. But these generations also received a solid grounding in the arts — both at home and at school, through arts education programming.

We are now witnessing the first generation of college graduates that did not receive a solid arts education in grammar school. As this generation of millennials ages, it is not at all clear that they will feel inclined to participate in the arts as audience members, donors, or board members. Even those younger people who are now arriving at the age when they can become donors are typically giving less than their parents did. There are exceptions, of course, including cases in which family foundations are required to give certain amounts each year. Even in these instances, however, many younger family members find it more important to give to social service organizations than to arts organizations since they do not have a natural affinity for the arts.

With contributed income playing an increasingly large role in maintaining the health of arts organizations, the aging of our donor base is of huge importance. Many arts institutions grew quite large over the past thirty years based on the support of a dedicated group of donors who could give substantial sums annually. At the Kennedy Center, for example, the largest givers in 2001 donated $50,000 per year; by 2014, the largest donors were giving between $250,000 and $5 million annually! Successful and stable arts organizations were able to create a cadre of these donors instead of relying on one or two. Relying on only a few major donors gives them far too much power, since the loss of one or two would be catastrophic.

Over the next twenty years, we are going to witness the demise of an entire generation of donors whose children do not exhibit the same level of commitment to the arts. According to the Porter model, this means the power of the remaining donors will increase — and arts organizations will have to do even more to please them. In bottom-line terms, this means that arts organizations will have less to spend on programming just as substitute products make it essential that they spend *more* on creating exciting and competitive events.

In response to this challenge, many arts organizations have tried to form young donor programs. The hope is that these programs will attract the major donors of the future. The rationale is that if we tie them to us now, they are likely to stay with us for decades — just as their parents did. These programs typically die of their own weight, however, since young prospects usually expect a high degree of service, do not make major contributions (they have far less discretionary time and money than their parents), and do not have the same level of commitment either to the art form or the organization. With relatively small staffs (and budgets) for donor cultivation, most arts organizations find that investing in a twenty-five-year-old today in hope that they will contribute significantly in twenty or thirty years is simply not affordable. With arts institutions under pressure to increase donations *now*, the decision to cultivate potential donors of the future or existing ones (who already give substantially) is easy. As a result, after a few months or years of effort, the young donors program fails, either because the organization feels it is receiving an insufficient return on its investment, or the donors feel insufficiently attached to the organization.

Because of inflation and the arts' productivity problem, the budgets of arts organizations will only continue to grow. For most of these organizations, earned income will represent a smaller percentage of total revenue. For those arts organizations fortunate enough to have an endowment, that means either endowment income or contributed income (or both) will have to rise. Over the past decade, we have seen many arts organizations raiding their endowments to cover cash-flow needs. In 2006, for example, the Baltimore Symphony liquidated one-third of its endowment to pay off debts and establish fiscal stability; by 2010, the symphony was once again asking musicians to take a pay cut. Other organizations also have spent far larger percentages of their endowments than is considered prudent. This mortgages the future of the organization to pay current expenses. Because endowment funds are typically given by the most dedicated and generous donors—and such donors are dying off—it is likely that many arts institutions will be unable to add to their endowment funds in the future. This means that endowment income, like earned income, will become a smaller part of overall revenue—forcing even more reliance on fund-raising. And because there will be fewer donors in general, the pressure on each one will be greater.

The aging of the donor base represents the most difficult trend for the arts to overcome in the decades ahead. The need for an increasing level of contributions, combined with a contracting donor base, is likely to drive many arts institutions into bankruptcy. Those few large arts organizations able to build a sufficient base—cultivating both nearby donors and those who may be thousands of miles away—will be able to fight this trend. All others will be seriously affected. We already see this division happening. While total arts contributions did not fall precipitously during the recession, they did fall dramatically for a subset of organizations.

THE DECLINE OF TOURING

Another aspect of the arts industry likely to change dramatically is a subgroup of competitors: the international touring companies that land for a day or a week, give a small set of performances, then depart. For the past sixty years, Americans have enjoyed ballet, opera, theater, and orchestral music from all over the world. The great European ballet companies and symphony orchestras have made regular appearances in major cities, as have a few notable theater companies (with fewer opera ensembles, given the huge cost of opera touring). What most Americans did not realize is that they were enjoying these performances at the expense of the taxpayers of other countries.

The only way that institutions like the Bolshoi, Mariinsky, Royal Ballet, and Royal Shakespeare Company could afford to tour the United States was through subsidies from their own governments, which viewed these tours as essential elements in cultural diplomacy. (The U.S. government also sponsored tours: both American Ballet Theatre and the Alvin Ailey American Dance Theater added the word "American" to their names at the request of the State Department—and in advance of lengthy tours abroad. One of the most interesting items in the Ailey archives is a tour scrapbook belonging to Minnie Marshall, a former Ailey dancer, which includes the State Department briefings for every country visited by the company on a Southeast Asian tour, just before the escalation of the Vietnam War.)

As governments in Europe and elsewhere reduce their subsidies for the arts, most organizations will try to preserve their art-making activities at home—particularly as they attempt to build larger donor bases there. Since overseas touring is relatively expensive—and we all know that cutting art at home is not a winning strategy—touring activities will feel more expendable. Although touring can offer prestige, it may be viewed as an unaffordable luxury for those organizations that do not raise money abroad.

With the expected decline in government support, it is unlikely that presenters in the United States will be able to pay foreign arts companies enough to entice them to travel. Presenters operate under the same financial pressures as theaters and ballet companies and already find it difficult to offer complete seasons. The decrease in international touring will result in a true loss in Americans' knowledge of other cultures. The arts, after all, teach us what others find beautiful and important. It is no coincidence that artists have led the way in many difficult diplomatic situations—the New

York Philharmonic's tours to the Soviet Union and China played important roles in establishing dialogue with these nations.

Access to live performances by arts organizations from other nations will be replaced, in part, by an increase in electronic broadcasts of international events. But only the most high-profile projects are likely to be broadcast and marketed. Events with less widespread appeal—such as folkloric presentations or chamber music, as well as new and innovative work—are not likely to be transmitted in this fashion. This will leave a serious gap in Americans' knowledge of their counterparts abroad. And because broadcasts do not foster the person-to-person relationships that touring encourages, artists will lose the opportunities to experience the responses of new audiences to their work and to collaborate with artists from different regions. I have yet to meet an ensemble that did not gain poise, understanding, and quality from touring to other countries.

UNIONS IN A CHANGING WORLD

Another segment of industry participants likely to experience future dislocations is the group of unionized artists: the orchestral musicians, dancers, actors, and singers who have benefited from union representation over the past fifty years. As suppliers, unionized artists once had great power. When contributed income was growing (although money was never plentiful, it was far more available a decade ago), arts executives and board members rarely had the incentive to engage in salary fights with their artists. In those days, it was considered more important to avoid disagreements between artists, staff, and board members—along with the possibility of a strike, bad press, and unhappy donors. Arts organizations wanted to present themselves as well run and stable, and any disruptions would reflect badly on management. As a result, union negotiations resulted in steady increases in artist salaries and benefits (but no improvement in worker productivity, of course).

More problematic, however, were the increases in weeks of guaranteed work. Most artists are paid only when they work; very few receive year-round paychecks and paid vacation time. Many typically were paid for a certain minimum number of guaranteed weeks, along with any extra weeks that the organization could schedule. It was in these artists' interests, of course, to increase the number of guaranteed weeks of work, and many union negotiations focused on this difficult issue. Arts managers knew that it was highly likely that any increase in that number would be permanent: who would willingly give back a guaranteed week of work? As the minimum number of weeks increased, organizations scheduled more performances to pay the extra salary costs. (This raised other costs as well—for guest artists, conductors, stagehands, and other production-related expenses.) In many cases, additional performances were not justified by local demand, especially for symphonies and dance companies. As a result, some organizations pursued more touring opportunities, even though touring is expensive and tour fees often do not cover the added costs (airline tickets, hotel rooms, per diems, and so on). When I ran American Ballet Theatre, we booked several tours that lost money in order to recoup at least part of the cost of the extra weeks of work promised to our dancers. The situation was not optimal, but it was better to lose $100,000 during a week of touring than $200,000 during a week of unnecessary rehearsal. Many of the financial problems currently being experienced by arts organizations result from an over-supply of performances—events that are produced to cover the expenses of guaranteed weeks of employment. In some cases, unionized artists are paid for weeks in which they do not work at all. While these excess numbers of guaranteed weeks were negotiated in collective bargaining sessions, it is easy to understand the current concerns of board members, many of whom have been contributing their own money at the same time they have been struggling to balance budgets.

After several years of substantial deficits, many arts institutions have become willing to risk the public-relations hit associated with pursuing a contract revision. In fact, many major donors, concerned that they have been throwing good money after bad, are threatening to withhold future gifts unless a substantial reconfiguration of costs can be achieved. Such donors worry that they will be asked to cover an increasing portion of an organization's deficit—and know that their children may not have the same priorities for giving as they do.

This environment has weakened the power of artists' unions, since some boards have threatened to close organizations if costs cannot be controlled. Union leaders can test a board's resolve, of course, and see if they are willing to withstand public pressure. But it is no surprise that numerous orchestras have seen wages fall 10 or 20 percent in their latest contracts.

As the numbers and size of regional arts organizations continue to fall, union power is likely to weaken further, and there will be fewer employment opportunities for union artists. Celebrity performers, creators, and designers, on the other hand, will retain their power, since they are considered unique. They will still be able to demand high salaries, especially when they are involved in performances that are broadcast to many homes.

We should expect a bifurcated world in which the largest institutions continue to pay very high wages to engage the most celebrated artists, while smaller arts groups use low paid, non-unionized, or even volunteer artists. Although there is already a wide differential in artists' salaries, that gulf should widen further. (There is some indication, however, that major concert and opera soloists may not command the same level of fees as they did a decade ago. This is due, in large measure, to the reduction in government support in Europe. In the past, American companies were forced to match the traditionally high fees paid by European opera houses and symphonies.)

Moving to this new world will not be smooth or easy. The decades ahead will be difficult for unionized artists and the organizations that employ them. One would hope for an ongoing, mature, and reasonable dialogue among the various sides, in order to develop a rational plan that maintains fair wages for artists while preserving the health of organizations. But history does not suggest that this is likely.

Unions are not the only industry participants that will suffer in the decades ahead. Service groups also will deteriorate as their constituent arts organizations weaken or die. Opera America, Dance USA, the League of American Orchestras, the Theatre Communications Group, and others all depend on membership fees from the organizations they serve. It is unlikely that the largest institutions will have an incentive to increase their support of service organizations to compensate for the loss of weaker members. After all, these large institutions will be in fierce competition with each other for artists, ratings, donors, and board members. Why should they collaborate with each other to support a withering field? This will reduce the level of advocacy for individual art forms as well as the arts as a whole, and may result in even lower government funding than at present.

THE FUTURE OF MID-SIZED ORGANIZATIONS

These projections for the evolution of the arts industry have the biggest ramifications for mid-sized organizations. Should they fight the trend toward becoming large or small and try to maintain existing budgets? Should they bite the bullet and downsize? Or should they attempt to become one of the major players?

Some mid-sized groups will attempt to remain true to their missions, to a vision that is neither giant nor tiny. These will face a difficult challenge to renew their donor bases as the current group of donors dies away and costs continue to increase. As their "natural" audiences shrink, they will have to produce art that draws new and younger audiences. Board membership, in turn, must change to reflect a new donor group. Some groups will either be so potent or so beloved by their communities that they will continue to thrive, but this will take a remarkable management group, a far-sighted board, and a clear and coherent strategic plan. And success will require a consistency in implementing plans that is currently unusual in the arts. A few years of mismanagement or lack of institutional focus could spell disaster.

Those groups that decide to downsize will acknowledge that they simply cannot find the resources to maintain their existing scale of operations. But this course is not without its own problems. These groups will face a multitude of pressures as they reduce their budgets. Staff and artists will clearly be affected by the reduction in the amount of work available. There will be a torrent of complaints from unions, members of the community who love the institution (but are unwilling or unable to pay for it), and the senior board members and donors who wish that things could remain as they have always been. (In every turnaround I accomplished, I was scorned by a small group who mourned the way the institution used to function — even if it meant that bankruptcy was always just a few days away.) Such organizations will require a clear operating plan that allows for becoming smaller while still remaining relevant, as well as a strong communications effort that explains the plan to their constituents. Downsizing doesn't always end well. As we saw in the case of the New York City Opera, organizations that downsize without clarity may end up being perceived as irrelevant; this can make it impossible to gather the resources needed to fund even reduced operations. In fact, it is often easier to fund larger projects than smaller ones, as the publicity and excitement generated by a transformational project makes people more willing to give. By 2035, organizations that downsized in 2020 may simply have disappeared. And it is not clear that many people will care.

Groups that attempt to become larger will need clear plans for building programming and financial capability in tandem. In this new world of mega-arts organizations, there will be several different methods for achieving scale. A few organizations have developed over a period of a century or more — the Metropolitan Museum of Art and the Boston Symphony Orchestra, for example. These groups achieved size and (relative) stability by building loyal families of audience members and donors. For this reason, large American arts organizations will be more secure, in general, than their foreign counterparts, since they could grow only if they attracted private support. Many international institutions grew large by winning huge levels of support from their national and regional governments. When this support is threatened, these behemoths will have to gather a new group of private donors over a relatively short period of time.

This does not imply that large American arts organizations will be entirely shielded from problems. It would not be surprising at all if one or more of the current mainstays withers or fails entirely, due to poor decision-making at the board and staff levels. Families of donors remain loyal for only so long; if the relationship fails for any reason, they will look elsewhere as they make their giving decisions. Without a steady flow of great art—paired with a strong board and effective fund-raising efforts—the future of any organization remains in doubt. The bankruptcy of the Philadelphia Orchestra (now happily resolved) is evidence that no arts group, no matter how illustrious, is immune from the pressures of dwindling demand and increased costs.

Some organizations will achieve scale through mergers. For example, the Opera Company of North Carolina and Capital Opera Raleigh joined forces in 2010 to form the North Carolina Opera. By merging their operations, two smaller institutions often can produce better art at a lower cost than they could separately, and also can benefit from the merged boards and donor bases. But mergers are not easy to achieve. The myriad choices regarding board and staff leadership, department and committee heads, institution name, and so on, all present opportunity for disagreement and a need for compromise. When the two organizations reside in separate cities, the challenge becomes even greater.

A few organizations will grow in the old-fashioned way: by doing such important work and marketing it so well that a large audience and donor base accumulate relatively quickly. While it is difficult to name an arts organization that has recently achieved this level of growth, both the Brooklyn Academy of Music and the Mark Morris Dance Company are examples of arts organizations that have grown faster than others due to excellent work.

It also will be possible to grow with a small but very potent group of funders, just as the Metropolitan Opera did in 1883. The Neue Gallerie in New York City, for instance, was essentially founded by one man: Ronald Lauder, who provided both a huge infusion of capital and a great collection of Austrian and German Expressionist art.

The new Broad Museum in Los Angeles is another good example of this type of institution, which often focus on a relatively narrow range of work. These may not have been particularly large organizations when they were created, but they are very well capitalized.

On another end of the spectrum, we have already witnessed the mergers of organizations that focus on differing art forms or functions. In New York City, the Bill T. Jones/Arnie Zane Dance Company, a modern dance ensemble, recently merged with Dance Theatre Workshop, a downtown presenter. In Dayton, Ohio, the symphony, ballet, and opera companies have merged to form the Dayton Performing Arts Alliance. In Salt Lake City, Utah, the opera and symphony merged, as did their counterparts in Sacramento, California. In all of these cases, the participants hoped that costs would be lowered, that marketing to the community would become more effective, and that uniting the boards and donor base would be advantageous.

The Kennedy Center, of course, is the largest example of this type. The original institution, opened in 1971, first merged with the National Symphony Orchestra, then with VSA, which brings arts to people with disabilities, and, most recently, with the Washington National Opera. The Kennedy Center benefits from the diversity of its offerings — the money earned on its presentations of Broadway tours also can fund the opera, the symphony, and its extensive education programs. While critics sometimes complain that the institution does not focus enough on any one particular art form, it is certain that neither the symphony nor the opera would exist without the support they receive from the Center's other productions, and that fiscal strength can be built from a diversity of arts offerings that interest a vast range of donors.

Merging two distinct institutions with differing priorities and missions is not a simple task, however, nor is success guaranteed. When an organization moves from being an independent unit to becoming part of a conglomerate, some focus is lost. And when funding is scarce, especially during prolonged recessions, the arguments over which art form receives priority, how budget cuts are allocated, how gala revenues are shared, and how public-relations efforts are targeted can become intense. Upfront discussions are critical to ensuring that the result will be a true merger, rather than two separate institutions sharing space and an audit.

A merger is not the answer for every organization. Both board and staff leadership must enter into any merger with the proper spirit and a willingness to compromise. They must also recognize that, in most cases, the opportunity for reducing costs is modest. The rationale must come from the chance to create stronger programming or to generate more income, rather than the ability to cut large numbers of staff. Larger arts institutions require more administrative staff than smaller ones, and therefore the cuts in staff costs are seldom dramatic. This is partly a result of the leanness of existing arts institutions: they typically are not rich before the merger and thus don't employ many "extra" staff people.

Mergers require both organizations to appreciate the need for melding cultures. Even small arts organizations can be characterized by outsized personalities—among artists, executives, and board members—and in the personality of the works themselves. Every arts organization tends to have a pronounced culture, and it is not always easy to force two differing cultures to work well together. This can be a particularly difficult problem when one organization is substantially larger than the other and appears to be the "winner." In such cases, the board, staff, and artists of the smaller institution may feel like they have been vanquished and will fight for resources, often in unpleasant or unhelpful ways. If the merger was required to save the smaller group from bankruptcy, merging can be more difficult still, as the healthier group may want the other group to feel gratitude when they feel only loss.

Mergers demand an overarching vision for a combined institution. The tasks typically include reaching agreements on consolidated performance, exhibition, and educational programs; joint marketing and fund-raising approaches; and combined staffing requirements. Agreeing on leadership at the institutional and departmental levels presents another set of challenges. Combining boards and reconciling by-laws can be especially traumatic if one board gives far more than the other. Even the relatively mundane details, such as employee benefits and office computer systems, can take a great deal of work and time.

Nevertheless, current evidence suggests that a large number of arts organizations will merge. Between mergers, bankruptcies, downsizings, and closures, one must anticipate a very different arts ecology in future decades. Although the mega-organizations may produce more large projects, most people will have less access to live, in-person events. While I expect a great number of community groups to offer opportunities to those artists not employed by the major companies, their collective output will be modest. The many years of increased arts education, arts accessibility, arts regionalization and internationalization that we enjoyed at the end of the twentieth century is likely to be replaced by a different model, in which nearly all will have online access to some type of arts programming, but live-and-in-person access to major productions will be available only to those with geographic proximity and the wealth to afford what will truly be a luxury good. In this process, the diversity of the arts will certainly suffer. Only the smaller organizations will be likely to produce works by artists of color; the young, the unknown, or the avant-garde; and less well-known artists from other nations. And with a less well-educated population, with many other options for entertainment at home, it is likely that our children will not think of the arts as integral parts of their lives and communities.

This transition will not happen all at once, but it is, in fact, already happening. No major symphony currently makes its home in South Florida (though the Cleveland Orchestra resides there for three weeks a year). Many mid-sized institutions are producing shorter seasons, while many ballet companies are performing without live music. The Puerto Rican Traveling Theater and Pregones Theater have merged. Only three out of the dozens of Italian opera houses are solvent, and the Rome Opera is threatened with foreclosure. We now have competing movie-theater broadcasts from the Metropolitan Opera, the Royal Opera and Ballet, Donmar Warehouse, the National Theatre, and more. And a tribute to Claudio Abbado was broadcast live from Italy on the Internet. (I stayed home to watch and imagine that many others did as well.)

Little by little, city by city, art form by art form, and organization by organization, we will witness an erosion of the scope and diversity of the arts. Each year, another group of staunch supporters will pass away, to be replaced by warm, wonderful, intelligent people who simply have not experienced the arts as a meaningful part of their lives. While these citizens may go to a play or a concert on occasion, they do not possess the passion and commitment to the arts that translates into generosity of time and spirit.

I am grateful that I lived through the second half of the twentieth century. I have been shaped, in great measure, by the performances and exhibitions I have been fortunate enough to experience. And I was not alone in this good fortune. I was part of a large and diverse group of both enthusiasts and casual arts-goers who shared many great moments of beauty and passion.

The arts world is changing and the children of my children will simply not have the same opportunities for inspiration and education.

AN ALTERNATE UNIVERSE

TOWARD A BRIGHTER FUTURE

— OR NOT

Perhaps a substantial change to the political, social, or economic environment will reverse the trends cited above. A significant political event, for example, could result in a radical change to income distribution, placing more resources in the hands of local communities that agree that arts organizations are important assets. Or an enlightened group of corporate executives could come to realize that the best chance of building a creative workforce is the implementation of an aggressive arts education program. We could see a wholesale reduction in costs or a radical increase in fund-raising that allow arts organizations to reduce the prices of their tickets so dramatically that online performances lose some of their competitive edge. One or several major celebrities could make classical music, or ballet, or opera cool. A few hugely wealthy individuals could decide that greater access to the arts is their giving priority and support a network of regional arts institutions. Or a new social trend could develop that favors group activities like attending a play with friends rather than enjoying the solitude of an iPad.

To be sure, other industries have sustained major discontinuities as distribution networks changed and adjusted very well, thank you. The movie industry, for example, survived the advent of television, though only after a period of great losses for studios. But the development of big-budget feature films, widely recognized stars and awards, and broad international distribution channels have allowed the movie industry to regain its financial strength.

Perhaps a more apt comparison for the arts can be made with live sporting events, which also have high per-game costs and have been dramatically affected by television. Today, numerous television stations broadcast only sporting events and sports reporting. In addition to the ubiquitous ESPN channels, there are golf channels, football channels, and baseball channels. The huge professional leagues virtually control these channels and dominate sports broadcasting. Division I college sports also are now a big business—the *cheapest* tickets for the first-ever college football championship game in 2015 are selling for $1,899. Each!

Amateur and local sporting events have a difficult time competing with these behemoths. Even in Division I, smaller conferences are essentially going out of business as their best "franchises" join the mega-conferences such as the SEC, ACC, and Big Ten.

In this environment, there is still some demand for local sports events. Minor league baseball, for example, is selling very well. But the divide between the big and the little is immense. *Forbes* estimates that the Dallas Cowboys are worth $1.81 billion today. (That is more than the combined budgets of the Metropolitan Opera, the Kennedy Center, and the next ten largest performing arts organizations.) As the divide between large and small grows wider, there is not much room left for mid-sized sporting events. If a team is unable to earn decent ratings on ESPN, interest will wane and declining revenue will relegate it to the minor leagues of sports.

Is it possible to stop the same thing from happening to the arts? Or should we accept these changes as "progress" and live with them? Is there something that can be done now to ensure accessibility, diversity, and sustainability in the future?

I believe there is much that could be done to stall the bifurcation of our arts world, to ensure that high-quality live arts programming remains accessible to all, and to give young artists the chance to perform. And I think we can create equal opportunities for artists and audiences of color and enable arts organizations of different sizes and geographies to remain potent and active.

The movie industry has been able to compete successfully with television partly because the addition of new technologies has made movies more spectacular. But the industry also has embraced new marketing approaches that make films—and their, actors, writers, and directors—as visible as possible. Every star and studio uses Twitter and other forms of social media; many have millions of followers. Award shows are more popular than ever (and there are more of them). Talk shows and reality television are used not only as opportunities to delve shamelessly into the personal lives of their subjects but also to relentlessly market product. Celebrity gossip is a mainstay of such shows, as well as fodder for tabloid newspapers, print magazines, and online sites. Movies today are bigger and better marketed than ever because of (not in spite of) the popularity of television and the Internet. Of the fifty top-grossing movies of all time, only seven were initially released before the twenty-first century.

While the heads of for-profit movie studios have different motivations than managers at not-for-profit arts institutions, there is much to be learned from the movie industry. First, create a dynamic, surprising, and exciting product and market it in many different ways. Then make celebrities out of your performers and creative team. And be relentless in building visibility.

BUILDING A FAMILY: THE CYCLE

The arts world is different from both the movie industry and the sports world, but if arts organizations could mimic the family-building skills of even the average sports franchise, there would be many more healthy arts organizations. Sports teams know how to make fans feel like part of the organization—and those teams are rewarded when fans buy both tickets and merchandise.

Teams feed their loyal base with endless amounts of information. As a result of their efforts, tens of thousands will go to great lengths and great expense to sit in a stadium and cheer on their favorites, while millions more watch on television. Although fans want to be associated with a winning team, many will continue to root for a perennial loser. Clearly not everyone who loves soccer or baseball is going to love opera and ballet. But if we could draw those who care about the arts as close to our organizations as a typical sports franchise does, we would have a much more satisfied and engaged family of supporters.

THE CYCLE

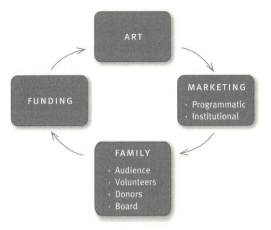

I have written an entire book on the tools required to build such a family. Creating great art, marketing aggressively, establishing a strong board, and pursuing fund-raising in a sophisticated manner will work to establish a healthy cycle that every arts organization in the world would do well to embrace.

If organizations spend more time planning exciting art—creating unique projects that surprise and delight their audiences—they will not be so easily swept away by online competition. A great choreographer, playwright, or composer—teamed with designers and administrators dedicated to making important art—can compete with any entertainment product. The only things needed are time and talent—the time to conceive and execute daring projects and the talent to make something unique and amazing. When organizations stop rushing the art-making process and plan farther in advance, they will be far more likely to accomplish something magical.

The Mark Morris Dance Group is successful because its founder has created astonishing work that is unique to his company. While it will be harder to build a reputation for excellence in the future, given the expected low visibility of professional criticism, it will not be impossible. Public excitement about a project now has the ability to "go viral" in a way that we did not experience in the past. Word of mouth is no longer the critical factor in ticket sales, it is word of tweet!

Works like Morris's *L'Allegro, il Penseroso ed il Moderato* are monumental achievements that cannot be duplicated by other dance companies, just as Ailey's *Revelations* is unique to that organization (and is likely the reason the company continues to thrive while so many others of the same era have disbanded). Audiences will travel to see great work. And experiencing *Revelations* live is different from watching a movie. On its extensive tours, the Ailey company routinely performs in sold-out theaters. I have watched *Revelations* create an instant community out of audiences from Tokyo to Toledo. The company—and its work—can unite people of many differing backgrounds and beliefs. That is a power of art that will not disappear.

The Steppenwolf Theatre Company's *August: Osage County* and the American Repertory Theater's revival of *Pippin* were productions that huge numbers of people wanted to experience. In both cases, a theater company took risks to do something different and special. And in both cases, that success has been repeated over and over again, establishing a reputation for artistic excellence. As long as they continue to create theater magic, it is hard to imagine a scenario in which these two organizations do not thrive.

But many arts organizations have been so frightened by fiscal issues that they have stopped taking risks. They are too deeply concerned that tickets won't sell, donors won't be happy, and cash will not be available; as a result, they have become too conservative in their art-making. They create works that are like other works that sold well in the past. And they start each project with the words, "How much can we spend?" But when one plans an artistic project simply to meet a budget, when the first concern is about resources and not about having something important to express, it is highly unlikely that the project will be transformational. When one replicates something else, even if that project was groundbreaking, one is still a copycat. Although television can get away with this approach, the performing arts cannot.

Rather than conceiving great projects—with enough lead time

to find the resources needed to pay for them—too many organizations are planning art that is inexpensive, undemanding and, frankly, boring. Whenever the budget is developed before the art is conceived, one is likely to produce staid, less interesting work.

Art-making is about dreaming. And those dreams are about beautiful and remarkable images, important subject matter that demands exploration, fellow artists with whom to collaborate, appropriate venues for the given work, and new technologies that could be brought to bear. Art-making is about artists with the unique vision to express something personal, with a vocabulary that is specific to them alone. When one asks an artist to dream of an amazing project—and then gives an organization the time to do it well, as the artist wants it—the results can be staggering. When David Edgar, John Caird, and Trevor Nunn conceived of an eight-and-a-half-hour stage version of *Nicholas Nickleby*, they did not begin with a budget. They began with an inspiration that made theater history.

When Peter Brook conceived of his spare yet beautiful version of *A Midsummer Night's Dream*, he was inspired by the words of Shakespeare, not the annual budget of the Royal Shakespeare Company. I saw that production three times as a senior in high school (and traveled a good distance to do so). It remains in my consciousness over forty years later. I cannot tell you about one television show I saw that year, but I can easily recall my experiences with Peter Brook's *Dream*, the white walls and the large feather. And I can assure you that I have seen every Peter Brook production I possibly could (and even presented a few at the Kennedy Center), all because of that show.

It has always fascinated me to know that some people will travel great distances to see works of art that they believe will inspire, entertain, or engage them in some way—just as other people will do the same for a sporting event that promises to be exciting and special. Attendance on Broadway has never been higher, and about two-thirds of the 12 million tickets sold are purchased by tourists. Of these, a full one-third are international tourists. "Ring nuts" (fans of Wagner's *Ring* cycle) also are known to travel far and wide to witness yet another production.

In the mid-1990s, I was a consultant to the Market Theatre in Johannesburg, South Africa. The Market is an amazing organization, home of the South African protest theater that changed the world's view of apartheid. Its founder, Barney Simon, produced and directed many of most famous South African plays, including much of the Athol Fugard canon. Blacks and whites worked together at the Market; famously, a black Othello kissed a white Desdemona during the height of the apartheid era. There were threats of retaliation, but the Market kept doing its work. Not surprisingly, the Market Theatre received no government funding. It relied on grants instead, particularly from foreign corporations and governments. (Foreign corporations were pressured to contribute to NGOs as the price of doing business in embargoed South Africa.)

By 1994, Nelson Mandela had been elected president and the nation was changing. The Market was challenged by the loss of private funding, which evaporated as soon as apartheid ended. Government funding remained absent, while protest theater came to a virtual end.

As the Market was not in one of the nicer neighborhoods — and a great deal of attention was being paid to crime in South Africa — attendance was falling. Some wondered whether the Market could still attract an audience to its precinct. But whenever a major American or British television or movie star was featured, the place would be jam-packed! People of all backgrounds, including a good number of well-to-do whites, would magically appear at the theater. I learned then that people will go to unusual lengths to see a work, an artist, or an event they think will be spectacular.

If every arts organization would improve the quality, the excitement, and the *dreaminess* of their work, the future of the arts would look very different. In that environment, each arts organization would truly become a specialty provider — there wouldn't be twenty ballet companies performing *Giselle* and fifty theater companies doing *Driving Miss Daisy* in any given week.

But great art also must be supported by great marketing. Too many arts organizations are losing audiences and donors because they are not marketing in an aggressive, proactive, and engaging way. I have found that most arts organizations under-market their activities. They focus exclusively on selling tickets and forget that marketing to donors is essential as well.

Selling tickets is critical, of course, and we are fortunate to have new technologies that make it easier and less expensive to do so than in the past. But the arts have not fully kept pace with the growth and development of new technologies. Although many organizations casually use e-mail blasts, Web sites, and social media, too few have truly developed a strategy to take advantage of these resources. Most arts organizations have a development committee or a finance committee composed of interested and knowledgeable board members, but very few have a technology committee that can advise on new uses of technology and provide access to expertise or equipment.

Technology is not a cure-all for the arts, or even for arts marketing. Without the right data and strategy—along with great arts programming—new technology can simply become an under-utilized (and expensive) toy. While the potential of new technology excites many people, including board members looking for answers to the income gap, all expenses must be viewed in context. If we are spending money on x, then we have to take it from y. Such trade-offs are never simple, especially when the choice is between technology and art.

It bears repeating that no marketing technology can take the place of good art. Too many boards focus on a new Web site as the answer for a struggling organization, even as the art is being pruned back and made less interesting. New electronic technologies do not *create* new audiences, they only provide access to information. If the work is boring, no amount of technology is going to save it.

Selling tickets is not enough. When General Electric ran its historic ad campaign ("GE brings good things to life"), the company was not selling a specific product; it was maintaining the prominence of the GE brand. In one study conducted in the 1980s, consumers were asked which company manufactured the best corn popper. General Electric won by a landslide, despite the fact that *it did not make a corn popper*. Marketing campaigns like GE's are sometimes termed "shareholder advertising," since the intended targets include the people who might chose to invest in a corporation. Nevertheless, many consumers came to think of GE as the go-to firm for consumer electronics.

Since arts institutions do not have shareholders, they are different from publicly held corporations. Like corporations, however, we have a great stake in the people who invest in us. Current and future donors will give only if they believe we are potent, exciting, and important institutions. When the only thing we are marketing is a ticket to next Thursday's performance, we are not inspiring the donor base who wants to know about our full range of programs, including those for which we do not sell tickets, such as education and outreach programming.

In my experience, donors may not even be interested in our art form — and yet they will still contribute to us if they believe we are of importance to their communities. I have managed several dance companies, for example, an art form that does not engage the interest of many corporate leaders. But when we explain the role of dance in the community — how many of the challenges facing young people revolve around lack of respect for their own bodies (teen pregnancy, drug abuse, HIV/AIDS) and how dance teaches respect for the body (and far less expensively than many social programs) — we can inspire them to contribute. Donors may only come to one or two performances a year, however. We need to reach them more often — with information and special events — if they are to feel as if the organization is central to their lives.

People are energized when they learn about the grants and awards we have won, the fiscal health we have created, the celebrity artists with whom we are working, the illustrious history of our organization and our plans for important new ventures. Communicating with a list of prospective donors about these special achievements, mounting historical exhibitions, hosting symposiums with famous panelists, and announcing the next season in dynamic ways are all methods of building excitement around our organization. None of these are included in a standard arts marketing effort.

Building visibility in these ways is what I call "institutional marketing." Because contributions are likely to become a far larger proportion of our budgets — and the competition for donors is expected to increase regionally, nationally, and even internationally — institutional marketing will become far more important in the future. Those arts organizations that do great institutional marketing will thrive in the years to come. (Of course, a transformational arts project is our best institutional marketing. When we create a production that the press and public can't stop talking about, we are transformed in the eyes of the world. This is what *Pippin* did for the American Repertory Theater and what the Sondheim Celebration did for the Kennedy Center.)

Strong institutional marketing also helps sell tickets. La Scala, the Bolshoi, and the Paris Opera Ballet all can spend less on programmatic marketing — the selling of tickets — because they benefit from their high institutional visibility, earned generations ago. No arts organization, however — no matter how famous — can afford to rest on its laurels. The Rome Opera, for example, is facing bankruptcy — and this was the house that offered the world premieres of both *Cavelleria Rusticana* and *Tosca*! We all compete for the same *new* audience members and the same *new* donors. If we are not working actively *now*, we will lose out to an organization that is.

But creating great art and marketing aggressively are still not enough to maintain a donor base. We also must welcome donors and audience members into our families, with open arms and open hearts. This will be especially important in the future, as fewer people will have received arts programming in school and will therefore have less affinity for supporting arts institutions. We must want to expand both the number and diversity of the people who care about us, and to make donor service a key element in the way we operate. It is astonishing to me how many arts institutions, while desperate to raise additional funds, make it so difficult for new donors to engage. Rather than welcoming others, they remain cliquish or remote or absent. Donor service will be especially important in a world where so much art is transmitted electronically and where there are likely to be fewer opportunities to greet potential family members face to face. Before each performance I produce, I typically stand in the lobby of the theater to welcome both those who are already family members and those who would like to get involved. Some of the people I meet simply want to make a comment about our work, our building, or our food. But taking these moments to connect to people who care about our art is as important as any membership brochure in building relationships. When art is broadcast into people's homes, I won't have that same opportunity. In that new world, arts institutions will have to manufacture events to bring current and potential supporters together. Those organizations that find creative ways to establish personal relationships with prospective donors are the ones that will see their revenue grow to match their expenses.

THE IDEAL BOARD

The need for open arms and open hearts is especially true for the most important members of our institutional family — our boards. Too many boards are homogenous groups of friends. Boards tend to be the least diverse when the nominating committee is composed of members of the same social set. It is natural that such a group will know and like the same kinds of people. As we attempt to broaden the base of those who care about our work, however, we need to build larger and more diverse boards. We need boards that have the power to attract funding from a broad spectrum of the community, the state, the nation, and perhaps even the world. We need boards that have the ability to chart a strategy, with senior staff, that will address the many changes our world will certainly experience. We need boards who can serve as ambassadors in a larger, more complicated realm.

For this reason, I recommend that arts organizations stop thinking incrementally about new board members; instead, they should plan for the "ideal board." Most boards add members one by one, as places become vacant or as financial needs dictate. Under this strategy, the structure and the culture of the board does not change — a new face or two is merely added each year. Unfortunately, this approach does not quickly move the board to a new level of potency; it only allows the board to evolve, slowly, over a long period of time. My approach allows the nominating committee and board leadership to recast the board in a new way to address future institutional problems and requirements.

The ideal board is a mix of people who are most likely to be helpful in the future. It is a description of the diverse skills and backgrounds we want on our board: diversity by expertise, by geography, by industry, by race, and by giving level. The list of skill sets we may want on our board depends on the strengths of our staff and the plans for the organization. An organization planning a new building, for example, may well want people with real estate development or construction expertise on its board. And if we hope to take advantage of online broadcasting, we must have the media and technology knowledge to do so effectively.

If we are serving a broad region, we will want a board that reflects that geography. If we are only a local organization, a local board may be satisfactory. But as many organizations will be attempting to serve larger regions, it will be essential to build boards that reflect this new scope. If we reside in a city with several key industry groups, we will want to make sure that we have representation from all of them so we are not leaving out potential contacts and sources of revenue.

If we work with diverse groups of people in our community, we will want a board that reflects that diversity. This does not mean adding one person of color to please certain funders. It means acknowledging that we are part of a rich and diverse community and asserting that we want to reflect this in our board, our programming, and our marketing.

And we will want diversity of giving capacities. Too many boards focus on a give-or-get requirement that sets a *minimum* giving level. I am more concerned with attracting board members who are excited to give more than this minimum. So I want to design a board with members who can give at different levels, and set explicit targets for these levels. My ideal board includes a few truly major donors whose annual contributions can underwrite big

IDEAL BOARD EXAMPLE

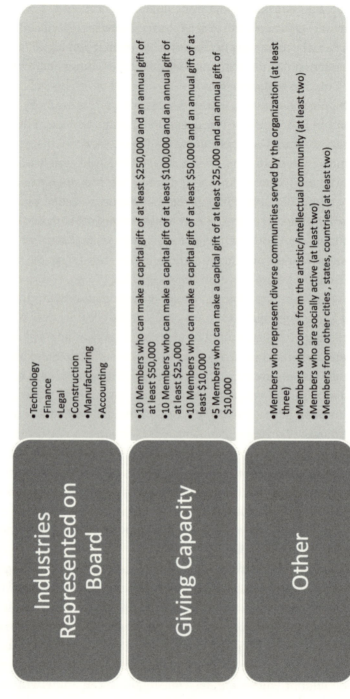

Industries Represented on Board

- Technology
- Finance
- Legal
- Construction
- Manufacturing
- Accounting

Giving Capacity

- 10 Members who can make a capital gift of at least $250,000 and an annual gift of at least $50,000
- 10 Members who can make a capital gift of at least $100,000 and an annual gift of at least $25,000
- 10 Members who can make a capital gift of at least $50,000 and an annual gift of at least $10,000
- 5 Members who can make a capital gift of at least $25,000 and an annual gift of $10,000

Other

- Members who represent diverse communities served by the organization (at least three)
- Members who come from the artistic/intellectual community (at least two)
- Members who are socially active (at least two)
- Members from other cities , states, countries (at least two)

works and education programs, others who can give large (but not major) gifts annually, and a third group who can only give the minimum. Specific target amounts depend on the nature of the organization and the community from which it draws board members. Board members in New York are often more comfortable with larger contributions than those in Philadelphia, for example, while board members of modern dance companies typically give less than those who sit on opera boards.

Finally, there are some special kinds of people we may want on our board: artists with knowledge of our art form, who can make connections with other artists and companies; intellectuals who can bring gravitas to the board and make board meetings more interesting; people with strong social ties in the community, who can attract the movers and shakers that bring excitement to our events; or celebrities from the worlds of entertainment, sports, or politics, who can bring a certain luster to our board and make it more fun to attend meetings.

After we have designed this ideal board, we can determine how far our current board diverges from the ideal. We can start to develop a list of priorities and requirements, then identify people who fit these requirements, just as we do when we add staff to our organization. It is at this point that we can solicit new board members.

At the same time, we also must determine who on our board no longer meets the criteria for membership. Just as we evaluate staff capabilities and ask those who no longer fit our needs to depart, we must have the courage to do the same with board members. Those board members who are no longer the best governors for our organization must be asked to give up their seats for others better suited to implementing our plans. This discussion must be held in a kind and supportive way; we want all former board members to stay in our family of supporters and direct their energies to areas that better suit their skills and assets.

In the new arts world, strong, well-designed boards will be more crucial than ever. The presence of well-connected board members —selected from strategic locations, with the power to draw others of means to the institution—will help build the family strength needed to thrive. We cannot simply add one or two heavy hitters to the current board and trust we are ready to face the future. In the 1960s, a millionaire was considered rich and a $10,000 gift was considered princely. Today, millionaires have morphed into billionaires and gifts exceeding $100,000 or even $1 million are routine. Arts organizations must learn to work with billionaires; they are typically short on time and only make major commitments to a few projects. Organizing the development effort to select the right tools for cultivation—and the right person to make the solicitation—are of huge importance. (Often, the attention of one billionaire is the best lure for attracting the interest of others.) Those that do the best job of strategizing for their development efforts will be the most successful.

Those organizations that produce important and exciting art on a consistent basis, mount aggressive and creative programmatic and institutional marketing efforts, welcome in new family members easily and openly, and create strong, diverse, and knowledgeable boards are the ones that will be able to operate successfully in the new arts environment. They will be the ones that make the new trends work for them, rather than succumbing to the changes in audience and donor needs.

Institutions that are already large and successful will have an easier time, of course. They already have the benefits of high visibility, access to technology, stronger boards, and broader marketing and fund-raising efforts. (That is why smaller, less successful arts institutions want to merge with them!)

But what about those arts organizations that are not already large? Is every small or mid-sized organization doomed to a marginal role in the arts ecology?

I think not. There will be some institutions, regardless of size, that will make themselves so vital and exciting that they will attract the resources they need even in a resource-constrained world. We already have a host of thriving mid-sized organizations: the Opera Theatre of St. Louis, the New World Symphony in Miami, the Pierpont Morgan Library in New York City. These important institutions have attracted a remarkable amount of support given their modest sizes. The Opera Theatre of St. Louis routinely produces beautiful and intimate productions of great taste. The Morgan Library holds unparalleled collections of rare books and manuscripts in a jewel-box setting; the quality of its holdings and its architecture are so stellar that many people are happy to support the institution. And although the New World Symphony is considered a training orchestra, Michael Tilson Thomas is such an important mentor and music director, the programming is so inventive, and its Frank Gehry–designed building such a great venue, that the organization goes from strength to strength. These mid-sized institutions have a strong chance of thriving into the future, if they maintain the excitement of their work and renew their donor bases going forward. (None receives a large portion of its funding from younger donors.)

But groups like these—whose excellence demands attention even though their size is modest—are in the minority. Most mid-sized and smaller organizations are simply not interesting enough to continue to earn support. To survive, many mid-sized groups will change the types of work they present in order to meet the tastes of the younger generation. Although this won't necessarily help the classical arts, it might allow the organizations to sustain themselves. (This reminds me of a group I once studied. The organization was an arts presenter in a major city; its mission was to break even. While not aspirational, it was indeed the board's honest goal. I suggested that they could achieve this mission by closing shop and going home. This suggestion was not appreciated.)

Having spent my career trying to fix troubled institutions, I know that every arts organization can be made healthy—no one lends arts organizations enough money to get into irreversible trouble! But those institutions that are troubled today need to revive themselves very soon if they are going to thrive in the future. To disagree with a famous American politician: it *isn't* the economy, stupid. The economy is not causing repeated deficits, cash-flow shortages, and smaller audiences. These troubles are caused by changes in demographics, leaps in technology, the rise of alternate forms of entertainment, and the lack of arts education. And, especially, by the lack of coherent and well-implemented plans for success.

Over the past decade, Opera Philadelphia has transformed itself from a struggling and marginal organization into one of the more interesting companies in the United States. It has accomplished this with a varied and vital artistic program which includes not only the classics but also a great deal of contemporary opera; this makes the organization appear fresh and current. It has marketed aggressively as well, becoming the most dynamic arts organization in the city (at a time when both the symphony and the ballet company were struggling), and welcoming new board members and donors with a warm and happy embrace.

TEXTURE AND SKILLFUL IMPLEMENTATION

Many arts organizations have attempted to transform themselves; some are successful, while others are not. Why was David Devan able to change Opera Philadelphia when so many others have tried and failed?

I use the word "texture" to describe the manner in which arts administrators approach implementing the annual cycle of building a family of ticket-buyers, donors, board members, and volunteers. Some managers dutifully attempt to plan art events in advance, to enhance marketing efforts, and to implement new fund-raising approaches—with little success. Their institutions seem tired and only occasionally interesting. Their boards remain unhelpful, and financial progress is spotty. Others, like David Devan, show remarkable results in short periods of time. The fact is that it takes more than the right vocabulary (or a good strategic plan) to build a truly exciting arts institution. It takes an insistent and consistent energy, a laser focus on key priorities, and an ability to embrace people in a way that works for them; it takes an almost maniacal fervor for the turnaround.

And it requires other qualities as well, such as the ability to read people and to understand what excites them. Too many arts managers are self-involved; they expect others to follow them blindly when, in truth, one must speak the others' language in order to woo them. Emotional intelligence is an essential asset for arts managers, especially as we try to solicit very large gifts from very rich people. Each prospective donor requires a different approach—and the language chosen, the information shared, and the nature of the solicitation must depend on the personality of the donor, not of the arts manager.

The mania to succeed must allow managers to forget temporarily the things that matter most to them; their goal should be to divine those things that are most important to the donors and to describe their organization in a vernacular that has meaning for them. I have heard many arts professionals refer to programs using terms that the prospect does not understand; although the names have meaning inside the organization, they only confuse the prospective donor. And when people get confused, they may suspect that the organization isn't right for them—or stop listening altogether. I also have heard the use of philosophical language that is unlikely to resonate with most donors, who typically care far more about how their lives and their communities will be affected than about the philosophical underpinnings of a work of art. (Yes, some prospects are very knowledgeable and involved in the art form; arts managers must be able to speak to these donors as well.)

Most often, I hear arts professionals and board members talking about the artistic reasons why a work is important—even when the prospect is a hard-nosed businessperson who evaluates success in different terms. When talking to most businesspeople, one has to be able to talk in the language of business. Focusing on embouchure, turnout, or other esoterica seldom works.

Those arts managers who experience the greatest success do more than just use proper phraseology. They also come up with creative solutions to challenging problems. They use joint ventures wisely, attract important artists, and dream big. They know how to package a project so that it seems large and vital. They can work the press, exciting journalists with their plans for the future. They know how to release information at the precise moment when it will make the biggest difference.

And they do all of this constantly, ceaselessly, obsessively.

Yet they can also be warm and personable; they know how to share tidbits of information and to make a donor feel important.

They are not always pressing for money or proving that they are correct or showing off special knowledge.

Although it may seem that I am going on and on about texture, there is a reason for such lengthy focus. After serving as a consultant to hundreds of organizations — and trying to discern why some succeed and others do not — I have learned that success is not all about strategy. Even more important is the manner in which we implement strategy.

This is not to say that every good arts manager has the same personality. Considering a list of some of my most successful peers — Deborah Borda, Karen Brooks Hopkins, Sharon Luckman, Brent Assink, Neil MacGregor — I can see that they all have different approaches to people and very different personalities. But they all are incredibly smart, able to speak in different ways to different people, remarkably focused, and terribly effective.

They also are driven to make their institutions as visible as possible, working both to create great art and to market that art aggressively. They are not all aggressive people, but they are all aggressive marketers.

More than once in my career I have been called a self-promoter. I never quite understood the charge. I do promote my organizations relentlessly and believe that is partly why they have succeeded. But I always thought that promotion was a critical part of my job. I know that if I had not pressed for attention, the Kansas City Ballet, the Alvin Ailey American Dance Theater, the American Ballet Theatre, the Royal Opera House, and the Kennedy Center would not have been successful, with revenue growth that outpaced inflation.

I remain convinced that if more arts managers were like David Devan or Deborah Borda or Neil MacGregor — focused on developing exciting programs, on marketing them in as many ways as possible, on engaging new board members, donors, and volunteers as members of the family, and on providing years of enjoyment and fun — the trajectory of the arts in this country would be very different.

While many Americans watch sporting events on television, there remains no shortage of ticket buyers for professional football, baseball, or basketball games. We can overcome a lack of arts education with a product that is astonishing, relevant, and remarkable, and an administrative infrastructure that makes it easy to participate. People should feel that their lives will be incomplete if they do not attend that new opera or this new play. If we can encourage this feeling, we can create the habit of going to performances and exhibitions.

TAKING COLLECTIVE ACTION

As fervently as I believe in self-determination in the arts, I also believe in collective action. I fear, however, that the principal way that we in the arts have acted as a group has not been effective. Our arguments have tended to be moral ones: we believe the arts should have a place in our communities, that artists should be supported, and that arts education should be available in all schools, because we believe that the arts are *good for us*.

Lobbying elected officials who care about the arts gives them the confidence to represent our interests. But moral arguments remain unconvincing for those who feel that the arts are irrelevant. We will attract more supporters through the excitement and visibility of our work than through what we say. If more people discovered that the arts could play a central part in their lives, then it would be easier to gain political support.

One way for arts groups to work collectively is to form joint ventures. These ventures can be permanent (to merge back-office costs, for example), or temporary (for a specific project). Whether by lowering costs or increasing programmatic excitement, arts organizations can benefit tremendously from joint ventures. Such endeavors come with some of the same challenges as mergers; they require maturity, time, and a willingness to see all partners thrive.

In several regions, arts organizations are developing joint online-marketing platforms. CultureSource, for example, is an association of 115 arts and culture organizations in southeast Michigan. Based in Detroit, the association has created IXITI, a new platform for promoting the many arts institutions in that city and the nearby area. Clearly it is of benefit to all participating groups when a larger marketing platform is able to provide a central resource for potential audience members and donors. This form of collective action could be especially helpful to diverse, avant-garde, and rural arts organizations, which by their nature have difficulty achieving scale. If a group of such organizations could create a major festival, for instance, they might achieve a level of visibility not possible on their own.

Sophisticated funders also could work in concert to affect the path of the arts. Rather than focus on individual priorities, they could develop a set of consolidated goals and deploy their funds in a manner designed to achieve those goals. ArtPlace, for example, was championed by Rocco Landesman when he was serving as chairman of the National Endowment for the Arts. A collaboration of several major foundations and banks, along with the NEA and other federal agencies, the program supports the development of arts-focused places in American communities. This multi-year effort has channeled substantial funds to this priority.

If a similar effort could support the creation of sizable organizations of color, for example, it is possible that some existing organizations could achieve a scale that would allow them to play major roles in the arts world. Or if a consortium of corporate leaders, recognizing the importance of building a creative workforce, could collaborate on an arts education initiative, we might see a different level of demand for performances and exhibitions in the future.

Another useful priority for a group of funders would be the training of arts managers and board members, since the deficit in strong management is one of the key issues facing the arts today (and the need for sophisticated managers will only increase in the future). Such a program could train arts leaders and board members to maneuver within a challenging, new environment, to build strong relationships with artists, funders, and other organizations. It could help develop arts leaders who appreciate the texture required for implementing successful strategies — arts leaders capable of creating truly successful organizations.

But to achieve any these goals, our funding paradigms will have to change. We can no longer afford to fund organizations simply because their missions are attractive; in a resource-constrained world, a proven capacity for implementation is likely to be required to qualify for large grants. And large grants will be necessary to help small and mid-sized institutions achieve their missions.

We also should take collective action to present our arts education activities in a more organized way. At present, individual teachers are typically left to decide when and if there will be arts in the classroom. This leads to episodic experiences that do not translate into a real arts education. Working together, arts organizations could create far more coherent programs. At the Kennedy Center, for example, we developed Any Given Child, a program that assesses the quantity and quality of arts education in a specific community, then organizes the groups that provide arts education. Rather than leave it to chance, educators and arts managers create a systematic path for arts education for all children in the community's public schools. This does not increase the cost of arts education in a community; it simply organizes the current activities so that they make more sense. The program has already been installed in fourteen cities and many more are on a waiting list. And the program's effectiveness has encouraged public and private agencies to invest more in arts education. If every child in America was able to access a similar program, the future audience for the arts (and the future donor base) would be far larger than currently projected.

Do we have the public will to tackle this project? Can we encourage superintendents and principals across the nation to give children the chance to exercise their creativity?

I wish we had a true arts leader in our government. Most developed countries (and many underdeveloped ones) have a minister or secretary of culture. A cabinet-level position could promote arts equity and accessibility, encourage arts managers and boards to act in proactive and healthy ways, foster joint ventures, and help steer a national discourse on the arts. This department could be empowered to create strong training and education programs with the Department of Education, strong cultural diplomacy programs with the Department of State, and so on. At present, there are nine different federal agencies which do some arts funding. But there is little coordination among them and much effort is wasted. Rocco Landesman tried to forge some communication among these agencies, with good effect. The presence of an arts minister would allow for more efficiency—and far more effectiveness—in arts policy-making. But I fear there is no will in Washington, D.C., to create such a position.

With or without a secretary of culture, those of us who appreciate the diversity of arts experiences in America today must act together to preserve our rich cultural heritage. We must educate our board members, support our arts leaders, and find creative ways to engage our children. Somewhere a child is sitting in a dark theater with his family, a child whose life will be changed forever when Marian the librarian sings "Goodnight, My Someone"—and her house magically becomes transparent.

ACKNOWLEDGMENTS

As I wrote this book, I was keenly aware of the many amazing people who have shaped my views about industry evolution, strategic planning and the arts.

I have had the opportunity to learn about economic analysis from Wassily Leontief and Ann Carter, about strategy from Walker Lewis, and about the arts from many remarkable tutors, including Martin Feinstein, Todd Bolender, Judith Jamison, Francesca Zambello, Barney Simon, Kevin McKenzie, Sir Anthony Dowell, Bernard Haitink, Twyla Tharp, Placido Domingo, Valery Gergiev, Christoph Eschenbach, David Hallberg, Barbara Cook, Stephen Sondheim, and Renée Fleming. I have had the counsel and support of astonishing arts managers including Claudette Donlon, Kevin Amey, Joan Rosenbaum, Calvin Hunt, Sharon Luckman, Bob Pontarelli, Lynn Thommen, Richard Shaw, Chris Millard, David Kitto, Marie Mattson, and Tiki Davies.

And now, at the DeVos Institute of Arts Management at the University of Maryland, I have a great colleague in Brett Egan.

The observations in this volume, right or wrong, are my own, but anything I have been able to achieve in my career is because of this remarkable cadre of collaborators and so many others.

I am indeed a lucky man.

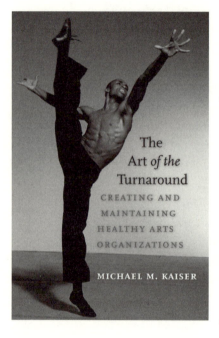

"[An] extraordinary book that serves as both cautionary tale and practical primer in crisis response. . . . Whether you are serving in an entry level or executive leadership position, from crew chief to executive director, there is much to be learned from in Michael Kaiser's *The Art of the Turnaround*."
— *Theatre Design & Technology*

"Michael Kaiser has a unique combination of artistic vision and executive talent that makes him one of the most capable leaders in the performing arts. This book tells the story of his impressive leadership. As my brother said in 1960, 'The New Frontier for which I campaign in public life can also be a New Frontier for American art,' and he'd be very proud of all that Michael Kaiser has accomplished."
— Senator Edward M. Kennedy

"Michael Kaiser, the 'Miracle Worker.' We know now we can expect miracles from Michael Kaiser, and in his wonderful new book he tells you how to do the same for your organization. Ten rules to his kind of success—that's what you'll find within the pages of *The Art of the Turnaround*."
— Barbara Cook

"There can be no one who has had the experience—the expertise—of Michael Kaiser in taking world-class performing arts companies and reinventing them for the twenty-first century. This is a goldmine."
—Hal Prince

"Michael Kaiser is an engaging and inspiring impresario, who truly has made a difference in turning around arts organizations. He knows firsthand of what he speaks."
— Renée Fleming

BRANDEIS UNIVERSITY PRESS
Published by
University Press of New England
Hardcover ISBN: 978-1-58465-735-4
Ebook ISBN: 978-1-58465-814-6
www.upne.com

"Michael Kaiser is very competent and far-sighted in dealing with the extremely complicated economic and organizational aspects of performing arts institutions, especially in this period of grave crises. In my capacity as General Director of Washington National Opera, which makes its home at the Kennedy Center, I have worked with Michael, the Center's president, and I share his approach to running not-for-profit arts organizations. I recommend his book to anyone who works in this area."
— Plácido Domingo

"Michael Kaiser has made it his mission to help arts organizations around the world succeed. He is an ambassador and trusted authority for arts administrators everywhere, generously sharing his proven exper-tise that I've seen firsthand. Michael's book will take his life's work one step further, elevating the world of arts management with his wisdom."
— Judith Jamison, Artistic Director, Alvin Ailey American Dance Theater

"No one knows more about arts administration than Michael Kaiser. No wonder people the world over clamor for his attention and keen advice. The Kennedy Center's not-so-secret weapon is an international treasure. The book is a goldmine."
— Terrence McNally, playwright

BRANDEIS UNIVERSITY PRESS
Published by
University Press of New England
Hardcover ISBN: 978-1-58465-906-8
Ebook ISBN: 978-1-58465-951-8
www.upne.com

PRAISE FOR MICHAEL M. KAISER

"Michael Kaiser blushes when you ask if he's a savior. But the president of the Kennedy Center is a missionary for the arts."
— *Morning Edition,*
National Public Radio

"Kaiser is something of a rescue artist." —*Time*

"Kaiser is the closest thing to a rock star on the nonprofit scene."
— *Daily Variety*

"[Kaiser] deliberately brings an outward calm into a situation where things are falling apart."
— *Washington Post*

The Cycle

A PRACTICAL APPROACH TO

MANAGING ARTS ORGANIZATIONS

MICHAEL M. KAISER, with Brett E. Egan

Practical advice, based on the notion of a "family" of supporters,
for managing healthy arts organizations

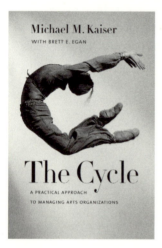

"The third in Kaiser's trilogy on managing arts organizations, this volume is prescriptive, straightforward, and realistic."
— *Publishers Weekly*

"Michael Kaiser has written an invaluable guide to managing arts organizations for success and sustainable growth. His clear insights are accompanied by a deliberate approach and simple tools specifically designed to help small and midsize arts organizations tackle what can otherwise feel like complicated and overwhelming tasks. Loaded with 'aha moments,' *The Cycle* should be read and reread as an ongoing resource that can be shared with colleagues."
— Anita Contini, Bloomberg Philanthropies

"Michael Kaiser has done it again: *The Cycle* is a road map for arts organizations that want to connect their mission to their financial success. The book takes you through a step-by-step process that allows your artistic strengths to be leveraged into financial resources."
— Dennis Scholl, Knight Foundation

BRANDEIS UNIVERSITY PRESS
Published by
University Press of New England
Hardcover ISBN: 978-1-61168-400-1
Ebook ISBN: 978-1-61168-478-0
www.upne.com